Managing Your
Personal Finances

Books to change your life and work.
Accessible, easy to read and easy to act on –
Other titles in the How To series include:

Paying Less Tax
How to keep more of your money for saving and investing

Coping with Self Assessment
How to complete your tax return and minimise your tax bill

Personal Finance on the Net
Use the power of the Internet to grow your personal wealth

Making Your Money Work for You
How to use simple investment principles to increase your wealth

Money-Saving Mortgages
How to take years off a mortgage and save thousands of pounds

The **How To** series now contains
around 200 titles in the following categories:

Business & Management
Career Choices
Career Development
Computers & the Net
Creative Writing
Home & Family
Living & Working Abroad
Personal Development
Personal Finance
Self-Employment & Small Business
Study Skills & Student Guides

Send for a free copy of the latest catalogue to:

How To Books
Customer Services Dept.
Plymbridge House, Estover Road
Plymouth PL6 7PZ, United Kingdom
Tel: 01752 202301   Fax: 01752 202331
http://www.howtobooks.co.uk

Managing Your
Personal
Finances

*How to achieve your own financial
security, wealth and independence*

JOHN CLAXTON
4th edition

How To Books

To Toby

Published by How To Books Ltd,
3 Newtec Place, Magdalen Road,
Oxford OX4 1RE, United Kingdom.
Tel: (01865) 793806. Fax: (01865) 248780.
email: info@howtobooks.co.uk
http://www.howtobooks.co.uk

British Library Cataloguing in Publication Data.
A catalogue record for this book is available from
the British Library.

Cover design by Shireen Nathoo Design
Cover image by PhotoDisc
Cover copy by Sallyann Sheridan
Cartoons by Mike Flanagan

Produced for How To Books by Deer Park Productions
Typeset by PDQ Typesetting, Newcastle-under-Lyme, Staffs.
Printed and bound by Cromwell Press, Trowbridge, Wiltshire

Contents

List of Illustrations

Preface
to the Fourth Edition

If we command our wealth, we shall be rich and free:
if our wealth commands us, we are poor indeed.

Edmund Burke

Insert 'money' for 'wealth' and that statement is what this book is all about.

As a result of teaching personal financial management to adults at evening classes, I believe I understand which aspects of the subject are of greatest interest.

Some of what I have to say you may already be aware of, but even with well-known matters, such as insurance, I hope to introduce to you a few ideas which are not common knowledge.

Furthermore, bearing in mind the size limitations for a book on such a vast subject, I intend to show you how to find out more, usually at no cost apart from a stamp or telephone call.

This is a book for dipping into rather than wading through from beginning to end. However, it does follow a logical order, with a chapter on financial strategy near the beginning which brings together and links many of the succeeding chapters.

The financial world is always changing and the information in the book can only be up to date when written; always check. Some figures are liable to change annually in the Budget. Where they are included I have used the word 'current' to indicate the need to check.

This edition includes the changes proposed in the March 2000 Budget, which might be amended before approval is given by Parliament.

I find the subject of money absorbing. I hope you not only profit from reading this book but also enjoy it.

John Claxton

1

Understanding Today's Financial Jungle

For those of us who have lived since World War II, life has become increasingly beset by doubts and fears and we look back with nostalgia to the halcyon days of the 1950s (or, better still for some, the 1930s).

First there is the ever-increasing risk of being mugged and burgled and of our property, vehicles and environment being damaged by vandals. This did not happen to anything like the same extent 25 years ago.

WORRIES AT HOME AND AT WORK

Our home is more at risk, especially for those with high mortgages. Negative equity, where you owe more than the value of the house because prices have fallen, is a frightening situation. And if we are made redundant, will our mortgage protection policy pay up or will the insurer find some small print to wriggle out of it? Is it better to rent after all?

Then our jobs are much more at risk. Everyone fears redundancy. We can no longer expect a job for life from one employer.

What about our company pension? The late Mr Maxwell, by removing funds from the company pension scheme, must have caused more worry, heart attacks and strokes than anyone since Hitler.

Personal pensions – and even the State scheme – are also at risk.

THE INCREDIBLE SHRINKING WELFARE STATE

We used to be able to look to the State for help when things went wrong. But now, in every direction – the National Health Service, sick pay, care in old age, unemployment – the Government is cutting back, telling us to look after ourselves.

This at a time when life-threatening diseases are on the increase – AIDS, a resurgence of TB, genetically modified food. There seems to be a new horror story every week.

The cost of State benefits has become so high that no government can afford to maintain even the present level without increasing taxation.

The National Insurance misnomer

Many people assume that their National Insurance contributions build up a fund, as a pension scheme does, to help them in times of need. They do not. There is no funding. What is raised each year is spent that year. It is just another tax and should be renamed employment tax.

The £8,000 crunch point

We must prepare ourselves for an increasing tendency for State benefits to be provided only for those in greatest need. The better off (who in some cases already seem to be defined as those with total savings exceeding a paltry £8,000) must look after themselves.

This applies even for care in old age, which is becoming of increasing concern. Even though the savings limit has been increased to £16,000 the property-owning democracy aimed at by the Conservatives, with assets 'cascading down the generations', is fast becoming a property-selling democracy, with the house being sold to pay for nursing home care and nothing left to pass on.

Do it yourself welfare

So your objective must be to set up your own welfare state. The trouble is, not only is it costly but also in some cases there is currently no suitable insurance available.

AVOIDING FINANCIAL PREDATORS

Even if you are fortunate enough to have surplus funds to invest, there are predators by the score ready and willing to give so-called expert advice which turns out to be better at lining their pockets than yours. Meanwhile the Government seems to retreat from imposing checks and balances, preferring an easier route for them – self-regulation: how trustworthy is it?

WHERE'S IT ALL GOING TO END?

No one knows the answer. This book attempts to point out to you the problems and risks. It will say many times over: assess the risk, read the small print, find out what is really guaranteed and whether the guarantor has the necessary resources and staying power. In other words question everything.

Studying the past shows that long-term trends are important. Many of the problems besetting us now have happened before and the tide has frequently turned. It seems reasonable to hope that it will again.

It remains difficult to recognise when the tide has really turned. Never expect to spot the turn: hardly anyone ever does. Instead be ready to join the upward movement when it seems secure, remembering that the further it goes the nearer is the peak and subsequent fall.

SURVIVING IN THE FINANCIAL JUNGLE

The laws of nature also prevail in the financial jungle. Your first objective must be survival and your second, growth.

In the real jungle, survival is achieved by knowing when to fight and when to flee. In the financial jungle, survival lies in recognising risk and being cautious, taking risks that you can manage if the rewards are worth it, but avoiding those you cannot.

Another way of reducing individual risk in the natural world is to club together – as do flocks of birds and herds of wildebeest. Comparisons in the financial jungle are mutual insurance, where each member of the club puts up a small sum of money which the club uses to pay for the individual disaster, and the unit trust, where the investment risk is shared.

So come on a journey through the financial jungle, armed with your compass of information, your whistle for summoning advice and your first-aid kit for dealing with complaints.

CASE STUDIES

Accompanying you on this journey are three sets of people:

Winston and Floella

They are not married but live together in Floella's parents' house, so their first objective is a home of their own. Winston works as a shelf filler at a supermarket. Floella is an apprentice hairdresser and is already expert in braiding. Winston also runs a portable disco (he specialises in reggae music and hopes to make it a full-time business), using an old banger for transport.

Alistair and Jean
They live together, having both been divorced. She has custody of her two children from her first marriage and they have a baby of their own. Alistair is a civil servant. Jean does part-time secretarial work at home. They own their house, with a £50,000 mortgage.

Gwen
She is a widow. Her husband Hugh died last year, having retired two years earlier, leaving Gwen with a good pension. Their three children are all married and there are four grandchildren so far. She does some voluntary work, using her car. They had reduced to £30,000 the mortgage on their £250,000 house.

DISCUSSION POINTS

1. Do you have negative equity on your home? If so, what have you done about it? Can you take it with you if you move?

2. Are you worried about your pension? If it is a company scheme, why not try to become a trustee, or at least get to know someone who is? If it is a personal pension, was it wrongly sold to you and, if so, are you doing something about it?

3. Do you know what your rights are under the welfare state? If you are employed, what is your accumulated redundancy entitlement? If self-employed, are you paying the National Insurance contributions for the benefits you require?

2

Formulating Your Financial Strategy

The purpose of this chapter is to find out your present financial position, first by preparing some background information and then doing a financial health check, which is the most important section in the whole book. As a result, some strategic decisions can be taken. The chapter concludes with a savings analysis.

PREPARING BACKGROUND INFORMATION

All financial advisers start with some background information about their client. Here you are both the adviser and the client, so it is necessary to start with some information about you and your present financial position.

Much of this information will be obvious to you but it is still worth writing down as it will affect what comes later.

Making a personal profile

The first piece of preparation is a personal profile:

- age
- marital status
- children by number and age and whether or not they are dependants; any other dependants
- whether you are employed, self-employed, unemployed or retired
- your marginal income tax rate (the highest rate you pay).

Budgeting

You may already have a clear idea of your weekly or monthly income and expenditure budget and whether you have a surplus to invest. If not, then the first step is to prepare a budget on the lines of Figure 1. Hopefully this will reveal a surplus: if you have a deficit then expenditure must be reduced or income increased.

Income   £

Pay (after tax)
Investment income
Other (*eg* benefits)

Total   £ ‾‾‾‾‾
                                                ═════

Expenditure

Home costs   − mortgage repayment
                 − council tax
                 − home & contents insurance
                 − electricity and gas
                 − telephone
                 − water
                 − repairs

Living costs   − food & drink
                 − clothing
                 − TV rental and licence
                 − social and sports

Travel   − bus/rail
                 − car − loan repayment
                        − petrol
                        − insurance
                        − repairs and service
                        − duty and MOT

Financial   − life assurance
                 − pension contributions
                 − credit card interest
                 − loan/overdraft interest

Special events − birthdays
                 − holidays
                 − Christmas

Other

Total   £ ‾‾‾‾‾
                                                ═════

Fig. 1. How to prepare a weekly or monthly budget.

A review of your expenditure may reveal potential economies. This book may help, as you may be spending too much on insurance or may be able to reduce your tax bill. Also Chapter 7 under the headings 'increasing income' and 'reducing outgoings' contains some further ideas.

Listing your financial assets

List any **savings** and investments you have, followed by a list of any **liabilities** – bank overdraft, etc. (leave out your mortgage, as this is not relevant to the immediate analysis, being of a long-term nature). The difference between the two totals is the value of your net financial assets.

If it is a negative figure, then you need to plan to reduce your debt (see below).

CHECKING YOUR FINANCIAL HEALTH

Now we come to the most important part of financial strategy, making a **financial health check**. The object is to check on where you are compared with the ideal.

Run through the following questions:

- Are you **borrowing money**, except against your house? (If so, consider paying it off as soon as possible as the interest will be expensive – see Chapter 3 for controlling debt.)

- Have you got a **cash reserve** to fall back on – at least one month's normal expenditure and preferably two or three, in a bank or building society instant access deposit account, or as a borrowing facility? (See Chapter 3 for accumulating an emergency fund.)

- **Disaster planning** – is your income protected by insurance against death, sickness or permanent disability of the breadwinner? Do you have adequate home and car insurance? (See Chapter 3 for protecting your income and assets.)

- **Retirement planning** – are you paying for a pension? (It is never too early nor too late to start – see Chapter 6 for pensions.)

- Are you getting all the **income tax allowances** and **social security benefits** you are entitled to? (See Chapter 7 for income tax and benefits.)

- Special events – do you need to **save** up for your next holiday, a new car, a wedding? (Putting aside just a small amount regularly is the best way – savings are dealt with in more detail below.)

- Your house **mortgage** – consider reducing it – see Chapter 4 for mortgages.

- **Education** – if you have young children, are you saving to pay for private education and/or university? (See Chapter 10 for school fees and further education costs.)

- **Investment planning** – have you surplus income which can be channelled into a savings scheme or do you have a lump sum for investing? (Investing is covered in Chapter 9.)

- **Estate planning** – will your heirs have to pay **inheritance tax**? (If so, consider how to avoid it or pay for it – see Chapter 10 under 'helping your family'.)

MAKING STRATEGIC DECISIONS

The result of the financial health check may cause you to reconsider the background information. First you may need to change the budget – if for example you need to take out more insurance or pay more towards a pension.

Second you may wish to change your existing savings and investments to fit in with the ideal – perhaps to put more into your cash reserve.

After all that, you may still have a need and an ability to save and/or you may have a lump sum to invest.

ANALYSING SAVINGS NEEDS

If you need or wish to save, consider the following:

- What are you **saving** for?
  - A 'rainy day', i.e. to build up a reserve?
  - To help manage regular expenses?
  - For a special event – holiday, new car?
  - For retirement?
  - For another reason?
  If you have more than one reason, decide the priority.

- How much do you **need** (if applicable)?

- How long will it take to reach your objective (if applicable)? You can work this out from how much you can save and how much you need.

- Do you need **quick access** to the money? If not, you can put it into a longer-notice higher interest account (see Chapter 3 under 'accumulating an emergency fund') or even into an equity investment, which should grow more in the long run (see Chapter 9 under 'investing in equities').

- Do you pay **tax** and if so what is your marginal (i.e. top) rate? Taxpayers' savings are taxed at 20% but those whose marginal rate is 40% have to pay the extra 20% on any income in the 40% band. Compare returns on an after-tax basis.

- Can you **save regularly**? It is better if you can, but be wary of committing yourself to a regular contract if there is a risk of missing a payment, without knowing the consequences. Irregular payments when you can afford them are better than nothing.

- Is the priority **income** or **capital growth**? Some investments are better for one, some for the other, but many equity investments achieve both.

- How much **risk** do you wish to take? By taking higher risks you may get higher returns, but only consider this for longer-term investing. Investment risk is looked at in more detail in Chapter 8.

Ideas for investing savings are dealt with in Chapter 9 at the end of the sections on tax-efficient, fixed interest and equity investments.

Figure 2 shows how savings can grow in different investments.

CASE STUDIES

Floella thinks about insurance
Winston isn't very interested in a financial health check. He says he doesn't understand those things. Floella is more practical and went through the list. She got worried about insurance on Winston's disco gear. She is already saving as much a possible for the 'happy day' and they have £2,000 in a joint building society account.

Jean is concerned about the risk of incapacity
Alistair has Scottish ancestors and is very prudent. Jean is more

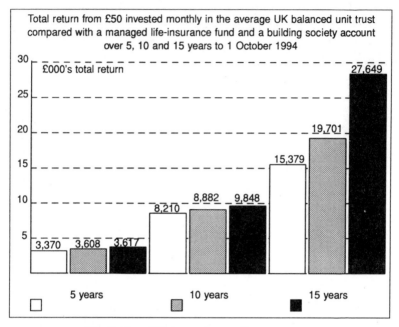

Fig. 2. How £50 invested monthly can grow.
(*Source: Hindsight from HSW, Micropal.*)

inclined to spend rather than save. Alistair has been through his own form of check and considers they are already covering all the necessities.

When Jean looked at it, though, she pointed out that, although he has life assurance through the occupational pension scheme, problems could arise if he ceased to be the breadwinner due to incapacity. They also think they should try to save.

Gwen worries about income tax
She found herself in good financial shape. She and Hugh took advice at retirement and she has investments of around £100,000 although these are due for a review. However, she has become concerned about income tax, as Hugh always dealt with it and she may not be getting it right.

The outstanding questions will be followed up in the relevant chapters.

DISCUSSION POINTS

1. If you are borrowing money (other than a mortgage) and you have a cash reserve, should you use the reserve to reduce the borrowing? What could replace the reserve fund?

2. The advances of medical science have made it possible to save the lives of people who suffer, say, serious head injuries in a car crash, but what of the additional problems this creates if the injured person is the family breadwinner? Do you have insurance against that event? If not, how much priority do you give it?

3. Is your mortgage sufficiently flexible to allow you to pay some off early without penalty? What priority does this have on your list of using surplus income?

3

Managing Your Financial Strategy

MANAGING BORROWING

Understanding the time value of money

Whether borrowing or lending money, the timing of payments of interest and return of capital has a significant effect on the interest rate. In the case of interest payments on loans, the time value is taken into account by comparing the **annual percentage rate** (APR). For interest receipts it is called the AER (**annual equivalent rate**), but is effectively the same thing.

See Figure 3 for an example of the time value of money.

Recognising types of credit

There are many ways of borrowing money. Of paramount importance is the **rate of interest** charged on the loan (the APR) but also important is whether you are allowed any 'grace' (time to pay) if you are unable to make a payment when it becomes due.

Bank current account overdraft
The **advantage** of an overdraft is that interest is calculated on a daily basis, so as your pay reaches your account, say each month, the overdraft amount falls, reducing the daily interest charge, and the average amount outstanding is less than the maximum.

The **disadvantage** is that the bank may withdraw the facility at any time (in contrast to a personal loan for a set period – see below).

A fee is usually payable when an overdraft is set up, in addition to interest, but banks frequently permit a small overdraft (perhaps up to £250) without requiring a fee. Watch out for monthly fees charged by some banks.

Unauthorised overdrafts can cost a great deal, in the form of penalties as well as higher interest.

APR on bank overdrafts is around 5% above bank base rate (the rate fixed by the Bank of England which effectively controls all UK interest rates).

When VAT on fuel was introduced in 1994, many people paid in advance to save the 8% tax. Decisions like this should consider the effective rate of return on the investment for the period.

Assuming your annual fuel bill is £100, what is the effective rate of return?

On the face of it, you might say 8%, because that is what you have saved.

However, taking account of the time value of money, you need to allow for the fact that normally you pay monthly or quarterly. So, ignoring seasonal variations, you would have only paid 7½ months in advance on average.

Consequently the effective AER (annual equivalent rate) of 8% over 7½ months is 13%.

Bearing in mind that it was effectively after tax, this was easily the best investment in 1994.

Fig. 3. The time value of money.

Credit card
If you time your payments well, you can get nearly two months' **free credit** without paying any interest. Otherwise, subject to the payment each month of 10% of the outstanding balance, you can have continuing credit, at a cost.

The APR on credit card loans is frequently 10% above bank base rate. (See Chapter 7 for more information.)

Shop credit
Some shops have credit cards which work just like bank and building society cards. In addition, it is often possible to pay for goods like televisions by instalments, which may even be interest free. If not, make sure you know the APR. There is likely to be a down-payment.

Loan from employer
Some employers are prepared to make loans, even if only for a railway season ticket, and they may be interest-free. A loan of up to £5,000 may be made by an employer to an employee on an interest-free basis without there being any tax liability; above that, tax is payable on an assumed rate of interest (but paying tax on the assumed interest is less costly than paying the interest itself!).

Credit unions
These are mutual societies, open only to people living in a certain area or with a common employer, whereby members lend and borrow money. Rates of interest to borrowers are favourable. You must have been a depositor for a period before you can borrow and rates of interest to lenders are low (average 4%, maximum 8%).

Further information can be obtained from the National Federation of Savings and Co-operative Credit Unions – Tel: (0191) 257 2219.

Personal loan from bank
Above a certain amount, a bank will not grant an overdraft but instead may provide a **personal loan**. The interest rate will be about the same, but of course is payable on the full outstanding balance and so it is more expensive. The loan will be for a set period, with a repayment schedule.

Borrowing against a life assurance policy
If you have a life policy and need a loan you should certainly consider this route, as the rate of interest is usually lower than bank loans and overdrafts.

Second mortgage
Because of the security, a second mortgage on your house will be cheaper – around 2% above bank base rate. However, there will be charges to pay and therefore this kind of loan is only suitable for the longer term.

Re-mortgage
This term is used to describe a change (in this case an increase) in your house mortgage. It is the cheapest commercial loan of all, but again there are charges to pay and so it is a long-term proposition.

Credit brokers
They can get you a loan, but beware of loan sharks. Make sure you know the APR before you sign anything.

Using a credit checklist
If you intend to buy something on credit or take out a loan, run through the following questions:

• What is the **interest rate**, expressed as APR, and is it fixed or variable?

- How much can you **afford to repay**, per week or month, in addition to the interest?

- How long will it take to **pay it off**? (The longer the period, the higher the rate of interest might be.)

- **Flexibility**: are you allowed to pay off early and what happens if you cannot pay temporarily?

- Is there any other **risk**, i.e. are you or anyone else being asked to give security?

- Are any **fees** payable?

- Is there a **cooling-off period**, so that you can think about it some more before committing yourself?

If you are not required to make regular repayments but have to wait till the end of the loan period and then repay in full, consider opening a savings account to build up the amount required by regular deposits.

CONTROLLING DEBT

Licensed debt practitioners will help you to get out of trouble with debt, but be careful because anyone can get a licence and any new credit they arrange might give rise to worse problems than you already have. Check the APR.

If you get into trouble with repayments, the best thing is to contact your lender immediately – they may offer a solution. If not, visit your local Citizens' Advice Bureau or telephone National Debtline; both will give free advice.

If you are paying extortionate interest you can get redress through the courts. You may also have a bad credit reference and if it is not justified there are ways of getting it changed.

Further information on all these points is given in Appendix B.

ACCUMULATING AN EMERGENCY FUND

Building it up

At least half the population has less than £500 in savings and 10% have nothing at all. Therefore building up an emergency fund is a high priority. The next best alternative is to have what in business is called a **borrowing facility**, that is a source of emergency finance from somewhere else. This could be, for example, a bank overdraft facility or a credit card with an unused credit facility.

The trouble with these facilities is that if you have to use them they are expensive (remember that the first step in the financial health check is to eliminate this kind of borrowing).

Another potential facility is your immediate family: would your parents, for example, be both able and willing to lend you some money in the event of an emergency?

However, by far the best way is to build up your own fund, out of savings.

Depositing it safely

Bank and building society deposit accounts are designed for money to be deposited and left alone for a period, in contrast to current accounts, which are intended for frequent transactions (current accounts are explained in Chapter 7).

Whilst deposits and withdrawals are easy, these accounts do not have the other facilities of current accounts, such as cheque books. A higher rate of interest is therefore paid.

A deposit account is a useful back-up to a current account, with easy transfer from one to the other. As well as being the place for your reserve fund, the deposit account can also be the first port for savings, especially for short-term objectives such as a holiday or Christmas.

You need to keep a record of the different amounts you are saving, but there is an advantage in placing them all in one account, as interest rates increase with the value deposited.

Understanding interest rates

Interest rates on deposit accounts may be fixed or variable, but the capital value does not change.

Higher interest can be obtained by accepting a period of notice before withdrawal, or an interest penalty for earlier withdrawal. Thirty days is a common period, but there are accounts available for 60 or 90 days, or even longer. Obviously more planning is needed here to avoid interest penalties and this may not be the best idea for an emergency fund.

Another important factor affecting interest rates is the **amount on deposit**. Rates frequently increase at £2,000, £10,000 and £25,000. There may be a minimum balance.

The frequency of interest payments varies, so rates are compared by using the **annual equivalent rate** (AER), which takes account of the timing of interest payments.

The final point on interest rates is that it is the after-tax rate which matters for you, so your marginal income tax rate is a critical factor.

Choosing an account

There is a wide choice of account at all levels of deposit and notice period and the situation is constantly changing, so what is best for you today might be different next month. However, when interest rates are generally low, unless you are making a very substantial deposit the difference will not be great.

One thing to watch out for is the closure of accounts to new entrants. This happens because the account has become less attractive and the provider has introduced a better new account. They are not bound to notify account holders, although complaints about this have caused some providers to tell.

It is wise to check the current interest rate on your account from time to time, especially if rates are volatile. Again the provider is not bound to notify changes.

To find the best interest rates check newspapers, *Which?* magazine or *Investors Chronicle*.

Using postal or internet accounts

A number of building societies have postal accounts. This system has enabled smaller societies to tap the national market without opening branch offices.

The **advantage** is that interest rates are slightly higher, mainly because the expense of maintaining branches is avoided. The **disadvantage** is the delay in transactions, particularly when making withdrawals. However, return is usually quick (except just before Christmas) because they aim to reply the same day, using first-class post.

There have been occasions when a payment for which timing was vital got delayed, but it is possible to plan ahead and use the telephone to check.

There are now some accounts on the internet, paying higher interest.

Guarantees

Bank and building society accounts (including current accounts) are guaranteed against loss in respect of 90% of the first £20,000, i.e. a maximum of £18,000.

National Savings investment account

A National Savings investment account is like a bank deposit account and is convenient for **small savers**. You can deposit a minimum of £20 a time. One month's notice is required for withdrawals or they can be made immediately subject to loss of 30 days' interest.

Although higher than ordinary accounts (which are dealt with in Chapter 7) the rate of interest is low, currently ranging from 4.5% for under £500, to 5.7% for £50,000 and over, but it is taxable. Interest is not paid out, but it can be withdrawn. See Appendix B for source of current interest rates.

PROTECTING YOUR INCOME

Do you need insurance to cover possible loss of income? There are a number of ways of doing this.

Protecting your dependants if you die (life assurance)

The word **assurance** is frequently used in the case of life cover, because death is certain, or assured. There are the following types of life assurance:

Term

This is the cheapest form of life cover, as it is for a limited period or term. An example is a **mortgage protection policy**, which will be for the life of the mortgage only. In the case of a repayment mortgage the sum assured reduces as the mortgage is repaid – reducing balance term assurance, the cheapest of all.

Another more specialised example is a **family income benefit policy**, which pays a tax-free income for the balance of the period instead of a lump sum benefit.

Whole-life

This pays out when you die and so is more expensive. Premiums usually stop at retirement. There will always be a cash-in value, but substantially less than total premiums paid.

The cheapest form is **non-profit**, where there is a fixed sum assured and a level premium. Other forms are **savings-oriented** but do permit the policyholder to adjust between life cover and savings:

- **With-profits** provides a periodic reversionary bonus (guaranteed once declared).

- **Unit-linked** has no guarantee and so is more risky but allows some choice of investment and can be very profitable.

Endowment

This is **fixed term** and **savings-oriented**. There will be a guaranteed sum and a cash-in value, but such policies only pay off if kept for the full term.

As with whole-life, there are with-profits and unit-linked versions, the only difference being a terminal bonus in the case of with-profits, which should be substantial.

So-called low-cost versions are designed to pay off a mortgage if you die or at maturity, without aiming for any extra amounts, which makes them similar to term policies.

There is a market in second-hand endowment policies and this should be explored in preference to early termination (called **surrender**). If your problem is keeping up the payments, you should be able to stop them and convert the policy to a 'paid-up' basis. See Appendix B for more information.

How much (if any) life assurance do you need?
Calculate it as follows:

1. How much cash is needed on your death (e.g. to bury you) and how much will be available?

2. How much annual income will be needed by your dependants? Take into account net income lost, less expenses saved. Will there be any income gained and/or extra expenses?

3. Calculate the lump sum required to provide the net income needed in (2) (assume a return around bank base rate and allow for tax) and add it to (1).

Statistics show that one in three people aged under 30 will not live to 65, so it is important to consider the need to provide for your dependants. A recent survey showed that six people in ten considered that they had too little life cover.

Life policies should be 'written in trust' to keep the money outside the inheritance tax net. Most insurance companies will provide the necessary papers free of charge.

Commission earned on life policies must be revealed to the buyer.

'Re-mortgaging' your life policy

Life assurance is currently much cheaper than a few years ago, when the AIDs scare was at its peak. It is therefore worth checking whether you can achieve a significant saving by starting again. London & Country (0800 373 300) have a free premium check service.

Accidental death

A separate form of life assurance is available covering accidental death, death from natural causes being excluded. Often some lesser compensation is included for maiming injuries, such as loss of eye or limb.

Premiums are much lower than for life cover, but it is difficult to see why such cover is needed for most people: death is as financially disastrous for dependants whatever the cause.

For other advice and for complaints regarding life assurance see Appendices B and C.

Incapacity and redundancy

'Incapacity' embraces both sickness and accident as causes. As there is some help from the State in the case of both incapacity and redundancy, these are covered fully in Chapter 5.

INSURING YOUR ASSETS

Buildings

Shop around to get the best deal. Think about the level of **excess** (i.e. self-insurance) you are prepared to bear, compared with the premium saved. Have you got security arrangements (outside lights and/or an alarm system) which can earn a reduced premium?

If your policy is linked to your mortgage, whilst you may be able to get a better deal elsewhere, you will need to get approval and there may be a charge or transfer cost.

It is important to avoid **under-insurance**, as this could affect any claim. Even if you started with a valuation and have index-linking, it is best to check the total cover every few years. If you make any additions, such as a conservatory or greenhouse, remember to add the cost to the total cover.

Are you covered for subsidence? If not, is there any risk?

Read the general conditions carefully. Do you know for how long the home can remain unoccupied before cover ceases? Does the policy include property-owner's liability to third parties (e.g. if a tile falls on the postman's head)? Does it cover workmen such as a decorator?

Contents

It is advantageous to have your contents policy with the same insurer as the building, as this saves some arguments, e.g. regarding TV aerials. But weigh this against premium savings by going elsewhere.

Types
- **indemnity** (the cheaper) which pays out the current value only

- **new-for-old**, which pays out the replacement cost (except for wear and tear on clothing).

If you can afford the latter, it is much better.

Have you ever been round your home, room by room, to assess the replacement cost of everything? If not, you are very likely to find it is more than you thought! Don't forget things in the garden shed and garage, and remember to allow for additions to the contents.

Does the policy require special declarations for high risk items such as TV and video? This may be necessary above an individual and/or total value.

Read the small print. Is there a requirement for special locks and security devices?

Optional extras
- All-risks cover for things you take out of the home (cameras, clothing). Is theft from your car covered by this extension?

- Money and credit cards.

- Legal expenses (note possible exclusion of building work).

Car insurance

Types
- Third party (the basic legal requirement).

- Third party, fire and theft (TPFT).

- Comprehensive, which adds accidental damage to TPFT and is of course the most expensive.

Factors affecting premium
- The level of self-insurance (**excess**) – usually there is a minimum.
- The accumulation of **no claims bonus** (NCB), which can usually be protected from one claim by paying extra.
- Car age, value and annual usage.
- Whether the car is used for work.
- The number of drivers and their ages.
- Whether you have a garage.
- Whether you have an alarm and/or immobiliser.

Points in policy wording you should check
- Does the insurer reserve the right to cancel the policy in the event of total loss?
- Is another car provided if yours is under repair?
- 'Knock-for-knock': do you lose NCB even if the accident is not your fault?
- How much cover is there for personal items stolen from the car?
- Are windscreens excluded from loss of NCB?
- Are the insured drivers covered when driving another vehicle? (If so, it will be third party only.)

The possible loss of NCB makes it necessary to consider carefully whether to claim for a relatively small loss, but any accident should be reported, to comply with the insurance code.

CASE STUDIES

Winston wants more disco equipment
He hasn't any money to pay for it so proposes to borrow from a moneylender he knows. Floella has heard about loan sharks and doesn't believe in borrowing money but she will not let Winston use their wedding savings either.

They have a joint bank account and Floella goes along to see about an overdraft as she has heard it is the cheapest way of borrowing. The maximum they can get is not enough. They can have a personal loan but it would be much more expensive. So she decides to get the maximum overdraft and let Winston borrow the balance from their savings.

She works out how much Winston can afford to give her each week, which will pay off the overdraft and make up the savings, including lost interest, over two years.

Alistair and Jean look at their emergency fund

They have an adequate amount in a building society instant access account. Alistair thinks they should go for a higher interest rate.

They consider a notice account but Jean points out that even a 30 days wait is hardly adequate for an emergency. She has noticed that postal accounts pay higher rates and doesn't think one would be inconvenient. So they agree to close their existing account and transfer the funds to a postal account.

Winston thinks insurance is a waste of money

But Floella is worried about his disco gear, which is kept in her parents' garage, and also his large collection of discs in their bedroom.

She decides to contact her parents' house contents insurer to find out whether the policy gives cover. Also the car insurer – does using it to transport the disco gear amount to business use?

DISCUSSION POINTS

1. If you know someone who has fallen into the hands of a moneylender and appears to be paying a very high rate of interest, what would you advise them to do?

2. Do you regularly check the rate of interest on your building society deposit account? Is it still competitive? Have they closed the account to new members and opened a more competitive one?

3. Home buildings and contents insurance is a good example of risk management – there is a small risk of a large loss. What steps can be taken to reduce both the risk and the premium? Which areas of 'small print' are particularly important?

4

Buying Your Home – or Renting

BUYING – AS SAFE AS HOUSES?

It has been said so many times that buying a house is the biggest investment that many people will ever make. However, it is not really a true investment, because there is no return – certainly no income; even if there is a capital gain when you sell, it will be needed to pay for a similar replacement.

When choosing a home, there are many more factors than the district you prefer and the size and condition you can afford. Experts recommend that the following be borne in mind when you have found somewhere:

- Are any fittings – carpets, curtains, etc. – included in the price?

- Are any alterations, repairs or re-decorating needed?

- If it is a flat or maisonette, what are the arrangements about common parts – is there a maintenance and/or service charge? What control do leaseholders have over charges and repair costs? Who owns the freehold?

The extra problems of buying a leasehold

There are many horror stories about owners of freeholds of flats or maisonettes charging exorbitant amounts for repairs in order to force leaseholders out if they cannot pay. Whilst there is some legal protection it is not enough, so beware.

The best situation is where the leaseholders themselves own the freehold. The Leasehold Reform, Housing and Urban Development Act, 1993 allows flat-owners collectively to buy the freehold of the building, or individually to buy a 90-year extension of their lease. To find out more contact the Leasehold Advisory Service – (020) 7493 3116 – or the Leasehold Enfranchisement Association – (020) 7937 0866.

The next best is where the leaseholders, although not owning the freehold, are responsible for carrying out repairs, usually through a jointly-owned management company, or at least where they have direct control over costs.

In the absence of control, it may be necessary to go to court to obtain relief from excessive repair costs. This can be expensive, time-consuming and not necessarily successful.

Estate agents
In England and Wales you will probably buy through an estate agent. Do not forget that they work for the seller, but their objective is a quick sale in order to get their commission, so they might be on the buyer's side in persuading the seller to accept a lower price.

In Scotland most transactions are done through solicitors.

Gazumping and gazundering
Even when you have agreed a price, there is a risk (in England and Wales) of **gazumping** – someone else tempting the seller with a higher price. This can now be avoided by entering into a conditional contract or lock-out agreement, whereby the seller agrees to take the property off the market for a set period and the buyer agrees to buy at the agreed price. In Scotland the system of 'exchanging contracts' in house-purchase is binding on both seller and buyer.

The conditional contract can be advantageous to the seller as well as the buyer, as **gazundering** (where the buyer later offers less) is also avoided. The National Association of Estate Agents will provide a draft form of conditional contract: Tel: (01926) 496 800.

You can now insure against some losses from these risks, at a cost of around £30. To speed up transactions, the government has recently suggested a buyers' **information pack** consisting of a survey, a copy of the deeds, searches and a draft contract. The seller would have to pay for it.

Costs of buying and selling
Apart from the mortgage (see below) the costs of buying and selling are met by the parties as follows:

	Buyer	Seller
● Solicitor – fees	✓	✓
– searches	✓	
– registration	✓	

- Stamp duty (only if price is over £60,000)   ✓
- Estate agent fee   ✓
- Survey fee   ✓
- Removal costs   ✓   ✓
- Connections/disconnections   ✓   ✓
- Installation of appliances   ✓

In addition, the price may include an amount for such things as carpets and curtains and there may be necessary repairs and/or alterations to budget for.

FINDING A SUITABLE MORTGAGE

The word **mortgage** was originally used to describe a document giving security over land to cover a loan. It is now commonly used to describe a **long-term loan** to help finance the purchase of a dwelling, although of course the security remains a fundamental part of the contract.

Most mortgages are **repayment** or **endowment**, but there are many ways of producing the capital sum to repay the mortgage. In all cases other than repayment, there are in fact two contracts – one to borrow the money (an interest-only mortgage) and the other to provide a lump sum with which to repay the loan at the end of the loan period.

Repayment mortgages

A repayment mortgage is where monthly payments of a fixed amount consist partly of interest and partly of repayment of the capital sum borrowed. Because this is similar to an annuity in reverse, it is sometimes called an **annuity mortgage**.

The monthly payment is almost entirely interest to start with and not much capital is repaid over the first five years. Those who move frequently never get to pay off much of the loan.

The interest rate is usually variable, which results in a variation in the monthly payment, but it is possible to get a fixed rate mortgage and this can be advantageous when interest rates are low. There are other arrangements available, such as progressively increasing rates (useful for those expecting their income to increase) and capped rates, where the variation upwards is limited.

Repayment is usually the cheapest type of mortgage and so forms a basis for comparison with other types.

Interest-only mortgages
Endowment mortgages
An endowment mortgage is two linked contracts. One is a **loan** repayable at the end of the period, on which interest is payable. The other is an **insurance policy** on which monthly premiums are paid, which is intended to produce a lump sum at the end of the period to pay off the mortgage.

The actual lump sum available at the end is dependent upon the investment performance of the provider, so there is some doubt about whether there will be enough. Many endowment providers are currently notifying policy-holders of potential shortfalls at maturity, due to lower expectations of growth, inviting additional contributions.

It may be better to consider an alternative, such as an ISA, expecially if you are a higher rate taxpayer within ten years of maturity, as additional contributions would trigger a tax charge on the whole policy proceeds.

Securitised Endowment Contracts (SEC) will for a fee of £10 project the probable maturity value of your endowment policy – Tel: (020) 8207 1666.

There are penalties for ending endowments before their full term, so if you move meanwhile, do not surrender (cash in) the endowment: it can be transferred to the new house and, if a larger amount is needed, you can take out an additional endowment for the extra.

If you have to surrender, consider instead the second-hand endowment market as you might get a better deal. See Appendix B under endowments for more information.

Pension mortgages
The lump sum entitlement on retirement under a personal pension scheme (see Chapter 6) is used to pay off the loan. Here there is even less certainty that there will be enough to clear the loan. Also it means that there will be no lump sum on retirement to use for other purposes. However, if funds are limited it is a useful combination of two tax-efficient arrangements.

There could be a problem if you change your job to one with an occupational pension, as pension mortgages are not available with company schemes.

ISA mortgages
The tax-free basis of ISAs (see Chapter 9 under 'tax-efficient investments') is used to build up the repayment sum. In this case too there is dependence on investment performance and therefore some doubt that enough will materialise.

Other
Repayment of the loan comes from some other source, such as investments. The lender has to be satisfied that the borrower will be able to pay.

Choosing which mortgage

The main factor is the interest rate. For borrowers this is expressed as the **APR** – the annual percentage rate – which takes into account the timing of payments. However, it may or may not also take into account other items of cost, such as fees, so to compare rates you need to find out what has been included.

When comparing it is a good idea to get a quote for a repayment mortgage, as this is usually the cheapest and forms a useful base to compare with other types. It is sensible to get a number of quotes for the favoured type of mortgage.

It is also a good idea to make thorough preparations for an appointment to discuss a mortgage, that is not only the information the borrower might need but also a list of questions to ask the lender.

In particular, find out about **flexibility** – will it be possible to make lump sum repayments and/or accelerated payments without penalty? (Some lenders calculate the interest annually, so lump sum repayments should be made immediately before the calculation is due.)

Flexible mortgages are now being developed into deposit accounts, where you can over-repay and borrow back at will, and even into current accounts, with cheque book, etc. Any excess repayment earns interest at the mortgage rate.

It may be difficult to get a mortgage for a flat in a multi-story block or one where less than 80% of the flats are privately owned.

If you want to buy but cannot afford a mortgage for the size of home you need, consider a shared ownership mortgage, where you buy part (usually 50% but it can be as low as 25%) and rent part, with a right to buy more in the future. Shared ownership is usually available from a housing association or local authority. Ring Shared Ownership Homes on (0345) 585 757 for an information pack and a list of homes available.

The best mortgage deals currently on offer can be found in a magazine called *Moneyfacts*. This is available monthly on subscription (£38.50 a year) but the publishers will send you one free issue: Tel: (01603) 476 747.

Voluntary CAT (cost, access, terms) standards are to be introduced around mid 2001, as part of new regulation of mortgage lenders (but not mortgage brokers).

Other costs

The borrower may have to pay for a valuation for the benefit of the lender. To reduce this cost it is best combined with a survey for the buyer, either a **house-buyer's report** (which is a limited form of survey) or, if the house is old or unusual, a **full structural survey**, which costs more.

If the mortgage exceeds 75/80% of the value of the house, the lender may insist on a **mortgage indemnity guarantee**, for which the borrower pays a single premium even though the benefit only goes to the lender, although there is now a tendency to discontinue this practice.

In this connection there have been cases where, after a borrower has defaulted and the insurer has paid the lender, the insurer has endeavoured to claim its loss from the borrower. It is advisable to ensure this cannot happen.

There may also be an **arrangement fee** – an additional fee demanded by the lender if there are any unusual elements of the deal.

On termination of a mortgage there are more costs – a **termination fee** and a **sealing fee** (the latter pays for the legal steps required).

Incidentally, when paying off a mortgage it is a good idea to leave a minimal amount outstanding – say £1 – so that it is easier to re-borrow should that become necessary. Also the building society continues to hold the deeds without making a charge.

Insurance

Except in the case of an endowment mortgage (which includes life cover) the lender may require the borrower to take out a mortgage protection policy, which pays off the mortgage if the borrower dies. This should in any case be considered unless you already have adequate life cover.

The other risks of sickness, incapacity or redundancy of the breadwinner should also be considered, as they may cause difficulties in maintaining repayments. As there is some State help available, these are dealt with in Chapter 5.

Changing a mortgage

If better value can be obtained elsewhere, it is worth considering a change. There will be fees to pay for early termination and for the new mortgage, but it is easy to work out how soon they will be recovered from the savings.

The negative equity trap

This term describes the position where the value of the property has fallen below the outstanding balance of the mortgage. The problem arises on moving, but lenders have recognised the advantage to them of helping the borrower to deal with it and most have arrangements permitting the excess to be transferred, within limits.

If you have negative equity it is likely that you are paying higher interest, the argument being that there is greater risk.

GETTING LOCAL AUTHORITY GRANTS

These are grants for home improvements and are either **mandatory** or **discretionary** (i.e. at the discretion of the local authority).

Renovation grants are mandatory. They are means-tested. Up to £20,000 can be obtained to meet specific minimum standards – for example, to install an inside toilet.

Disabled facility grants are also mandatory, but the recipient must be registered disabled. Grants are provided for the installation of aids such as handrails.

Home repair assistance is discretionary. The recipient must be at least 60 or in receipt of an income-related benefit. Up to £1,000 can be obtained for such things as insulation, or facilities for over 60s to stay put in their home or to move into someone else's.

There are also grants for landlords and tenants.

For further information see Department of the Environment booklet *House Renovation Grants*, available from your local council.

RENTING – BETTER THAN BUYING?

Renting involves no investment, so no tax-free capital gain but on the other hand no loss and in particular no negative equity, so it has its advantages. You know exactly where you are, providing that rent increases are controlled and there is security of tenure under the Landlord and Tenants Acts.

Problems can arise with flats, in respect of common parts, maintenance and service charges.

A booklet called *What Every Landlord and Tenant Should Ask* can be obtained from the Association of Residential Letting Agents – Tel: (01494) 431 680.

Taking into account the relatively low cost of mortgage interest compared with other forms of borrowing, the past history of inflation increasing the value of the home in the long run and the problems caused by landlords, many people still favour buying to renting.

CASE STUDIES

Winston and Floella look for a home

Floella takes Winston to the building society to see about a mortgage. They suggest an endowment but Floella says she has heard that repayment mortgages are cheapest.

The society prepares various sets of figures, which would support a mortgage of the size they need. Floella sensibly checks that the proposals are flexible so that they would be able to change to a different basis at some time in the future, or pay off extra.

They realise they will have to make regular payments once they start but Floella is now fully qualified and able to earn higher regular money, leaving Winston's disco earnings as a sort of variable bonus.

Bill has a mortgage problem

Bill is a self-employed decorator doing some work for Jean. Over a cup of coffee he tells her that he wants to buy his council house but is having difficulty in getting a mortgage from a building society because his earnings are so variable.

She suggests he needs professional help and tells him that she has heard somewhere of people called mortgage brokers who know how to overcome such problems. They have a look in *Yellow Pages* and find some.

Next week Bill thanks her, as he has been along to see one and there is hope, as it appears that there are some banks who will provide mortgages in such situations, albeit a little more expensive.

Gwen thinks about moving

Since Hugh died the house has become too big and in any case Gwen feels rather isolated in the country, so she is thinking about a flat in town. Never having lived in a flat, she talks to a friend and hears for the first time about the potential problems of leasehold. She resolves that she will only buy a flat if she can also own the freehold and have a part in the control of repairs through a tenants' association.

As she is getting on in years, she also thinks about the possibility of sheltered accommodation, where there is a warden to keep an eye on the occupants and help with any difficulties due to frailty.

She now has a specification to give to the estate agents in the town and as there is no hurry she can afford to pick and choose.

DISCUSSION POINTS

1. Does it really matter if house prices go down, when it is no more than a movement in the value of land and relative prices remain the same? Also the costs of buying and selling are lower. What are the arguments against this philosophy?

2. Which type of mortgage do you prefer: the simple repayment basis, where the only risk is an adverse movement in interest rates, or the interest-only kind with repayment by endowment, pension scheme cash or ISA? What is the further risk/reward involved in the latter?

3. If you want to live in a flat or maisonette, would you prefer to buy or rent? What protection would you look for in each case?

5

Creating Your Own Welfare State

REPLACING THE NATIONAL HEALTH SERVICE

As indicated in the introduction, the National Health Service is being cut back all the time, as expenses rise, in order to keep total costs from exceeding what the government of the day thinks the taxpayer is prepared to finance. So it is necessary to consider alternatives.

Insuring for private medical care

There are two basic types of cover, **NHS delay** and **immediate**.

NHS delay pays the cost of private treatment if the NHS cannot provide treatment within a specified time, usually six weeks. It is therefore much cheaper than immediate cover, as clearly emergencies do not need to be covered (in any case, in the event of an emergency you usually start off in an NHS hospital).

Points to consider

- Are pre-existing medical conditions covered (usually not and this may be important if you are considering a change)?

- Is renewability guaranteed?

- Are chronic illnesses (those which recur) excluded?

- What are the limits on amount of cover, for one event and annually?

There is usually a choice of hospital type, the most expensive of three types being London teaching hospitals.

Premiums usually escalate with age. Discounts are frequently available to groups, such as the employees of a company or members of a professional body. If the employer pays the premium it becomes a taxable benefit.

A free copy of a survey and a range of quotes is available from Tribune (independent financial advisers), who say premiums vary threefold. Tel: (020) 7467 3000.

Dental care is usually excluded. Cover is available but often excludes the cost of a 'full set'. Bearing in mind the theory of insurance, dental costs other than a full set of false teeth are not disastrous, so insurance may not be worth the cost.

Paying for care in old age

The National Health Service has already virtually opted out of long-term **care for the elderly** and some alternative is necessary. At present one in six retired people end up in some form of care.

Currently the State meets the cost of nursing home care up to a limit, but only if your assets do not exceed £16,000. Even then, there is a proportional reduction if assets exceed £10,000. The house is excluded from the asset total only if your spouse is still living there.

A recent Royal Commission has recommended that the care element of the cost be split off and paid for by the State, but will the Government take action?

Attendance allowance

People going into a nursing home will almost certainly be entitled to another State benefit – the **attendance allowance**. This is payable at two levels, the lower amount if you need help either by day or by night and the higher if you need both.

The current amounts are shown in the relevant benefits leaflet – see Appendix B. They are tax-free and there are no income or savings limits. For a free fact-pack on paying for long-term care write to: Nursing Home Fees Agency, Freepost, Old Bank House, 95 London Road, Headington, Oxford OX3 9AE, or ring their helpline on 0800 99 88 33.

Insurance

Care for the elderly is a fairly new area of insurance and consequently may carry volatile premiums. In true insurance tradition, someone has now come up with a euphemistic name – 'well-being' insurance!

The basis currently used to qualify for benefit is not very satisfactory – usually six standards of incapacity have been set and you need to achieve (or is it fail?) three to qualify.

Premiums increase with age whenever you start. Obviously it is much cheaper for the young because the need is rare. The average

age for need is 80 and currently the premium for a 75-year-old man for a benefit of £10,000 a year is around £100 a month (but 60% more for a woman). Benefits are free of tax.

Another way of taking out cover is to pay a once-off premium. For men in their 70s this will currently cost up to the equivalent of one year's benefit: for women it is twice as much.

As this insurance is so expensive, it is best to consider it as a top-up to income, including attendance allowance and if necessary what can be raised from the home (see Chapter 7 under 'increasing income').

FACING UP TO POSSIBLE INCAPACITY

As already explained, the term 'incapacity' embraces both sickness and accident.

Getting help from the State
Sick pay
Your employer (if you are employed) is required to pay **statutory sick pay** (SSP). It continues for the first six months of sickness (with rules about linkage to a previous period). The amount is currently £54.55 if pay is at least £61 a week. SSP is taxable.

Incapacity benefit
This has replaced the former sickness and invalidity benefits. It is tax free. Claimants must undergo a medical check.

There is a short-term lower rate of benefit for 28 weeks, followed by a short-term higher rate benefit for weeks 29–52, after which a long-term rate commences. The current amounts are £48.40, £57.70 and £64.70 respectively. There are higher amounts in all cases if you have an adult or child dependant or a spouse over the age of 60. Amounts change every year and are shown in leaflet FB28, see Appendix B.

The benefit is not paid while you are in receipt of Statutory Sick Pay (SSP) from your employer, nor if you are capable of any work (i.e. not just your previous work).

Help with housing costs
The State also gives help with mortgage interest payments and certain other housing costs if you are out of work, but this has been severely cut back.

Firstly, in order to get any help at all you must be eligible for **income support**, which means that your savings must be less than £8,000. For further information on income support see Chapter 7 under 'benefiting from social security'.

For new mortgages and other costs which began since October 1995 there is no help for the first 39 weeks. In earlier cases the initial period of no help is eight weeks, with only half allowable costs for the next 18 weeks. Thereafter all allowable costs are claimable.

Also the maximum amount of mortgage on which help is given is £100,000. Remember that there is no help with capital repayments.

Insuring against incapacity
If the State benefit is insufficient, consider insurance.

Sickness insurance
If the State benefit would not be enough, does your employer have a **sick pay scheme** apart from SSP? If not, does your trade union? If you are not in a union, then consider joining a friendly society scheme. These schemes normally cover loss of income due to sickness or accident and are for a limited period only.

In addition, insurance is available to cover the combined causes of accident, sickness and unemployment, which might be more appropriate anyway. It is usually for a limited period only. Benefits from incapacity insurance are free of tax.

Credit insurance
The purpose of this insurance is to cover the risk of not being able to pay interest on a loan (such as a mortgage, when it is called a mortgage protection policy) in the event of loss of income due to disability, illness or redundancy.

It is expensive (costing about £15 a month for a £30,000 mortgage) but as State help on mortgages taken out after 1 October 1995 is delayed for nine months, unless you can manage on savings it may be necessary to take out insurance for that initial period.

There are currently some problems with this type of insurance. Firstly, it is not available to self-employed people. Secondly, questions can arise on redundancy, especially in the case of 'voluntary' redundancy and also if you subsequently take part-time work. It is particularly important to find out what are the conditions for payment in respect of redundancy. Also check whether pre-existing health conditions are covered.

Permanent health insurance
Like many insurances, the name means the opposite. Life insurance is really death insurance and permanent health insurance is for permanent sickness, which can have a devastating effect if you have dependants. (You are 14 times more likely to be off work for more than six months than you are to die before 65.)

Usually there is a deferred period of six months, during which your employer (if you have one) pays statutory sick pay, at least. Then cover can extend to two-thirds of pay (plus pension contributions), with limited inflation-proofing, till normal retirement age. Benefits are tax-free, except for company financed schemes, where benefits are taxable after the first twelve months.

Some employers provide cover for senior employees. If it is not available to you, consider taking out your own policy. On the basis outlined above, the annual premium is roughly equal to the monthly benefit. Make sure the cover is on the basis of 'own occupation' and not 'any job'.

Critical illness (sometimes called dread diseases)
This insurance pays a lump sum if you contract one of a specified list of potentially terminal illnesses, such as cancer. You might consider that a combination of life assurance (see Chapter 3 under 'protecting income') and permanent health (see above) is better as the coverage is wider.

PREPARING FOR POSSIBLE REDUNDANCY

Redundancy is a traumatic experience which is becoming increasingly common. It is therefore sound financial sense to make some preparations in case it happens to you.

Availability of State help
Statutory redundancy pay
The State makes provision for statutory redundancy pay from your employer if you have been employed for at least two years. It is based on age during and length of service and level of pay at the time of redundancy. The maximum level of pay is currently £220 a week and the maximum number of weeks is 30, so the most anyone can get is £6,600.

The rate per year of service is stepped – half a week per year worked below the age of 22, 1 week from 22 to 39 and 1 ½ weeks at age 40 upwards.

Redundancy as recognised by the State only arises in respect of employees. There is no help for the self-employed.

Job-seekers allowance
Since April 1996 the unemployment benefit has been changed to a **job-seekers allowance** and it is limited to six months. The current amount is £50.35 (£79 for a couple) if aged 25 or over.

The allowance is only available to those who have been paying class 1 National Insurance contributions, which excludes the self-employed. Other benefits are available to the unemployed, such as **income support**, which also substitutes for the allowance after the first six months. For further information see Appendix B under 'benefits'.

Help with housing costs
This is available for people out of work due to redundancy. Details are given in the previous section on incapacity.

Taking out insurance
Credit insurance
Credit insurance can be taken out to provide for mortgage (or any other) interest payments following redundancy, sickness or accident, but not redundancy by itself. It has already been dealt with in the previous section on incapacity.

Unemployment insurance
No separate insurance is currently available for the provision of income during unemployment, although this may change. However, as already mentioned, there are policies which cover accident and sickness as well as unemployment.

Coping with redundancy
First you need to be quite sure you have received sufficient compensation. Statutory redundancy pay is the minimum. Does your contract of employment entitle you to more? Get advice from your trade union or professional body or the Citizens' Advice Bureau.

Find out where you stand regarding your pension. Can you take early retirement?

Make sure you have a letter stating that you have been made redundant and take it with you when you register as unemployed, which should be done **immediately** in order to maintain full National Insurance cover.

Where do you stand regarding your mortgage (or any other outstanding debt such as credit card borrowing)? Talk to the lender as soon as possible, to see what can be done.

Using redundancy pay wisely
The first £30,000 of compensation is likely to be tax-free (the golden handshake). Any amount above that should be considered (before you leave) for addition to your pension, since that would be tax-advantageous. But of course you may need all the money to live on.

You need to consider whether you have lost any necessary insurance cover which went with your employment, such as life assurance or perhaps medical, and consider spending some redundancy money to replace it.

Draw up a budget of income and expenditure. This will show how long your compensation will last.

Put the compensation money in a bank or building society instant access account (see Chapter 3 under 'emergency fund') whilst deciding how to use it, and get advice about investing.

Getting back to work
Finding another job must come first. Did you get any help from your previous employer? Sometimes a redundancy package will include payment of a fee for an **outplacement** service (one specialising in helping people to find another job).

You can of course pay for outplacement yourself. Certainly there is a lot to be said for getting some help, at least in preparing a CV (*curriculum vitae* – a brief account of your previous career) which is a most important document.

If you belong to a professional body, see what help they can give. It may only be that they circulate a list of members looking for work, but that is better than nothing.

Then it becomes a hard grind of researching vacancies and submitting applications. It can be discouraging, but don't go into a decline; you may have to work harder at finding another job than when you were in employment, so treat it like work, getting up at the usual time and spending the day gainfully.

It may be that changing your occupation would increase your chances of finding work. You could consider some training – numerous schemes are available to the unemployed.

Becoming self-employed

The alternative is self-employment, which opens up many possibilities, including investment of your redundancy money in some venture. **Be very careful** to choose something you understand. Some people have a long-term hobby which can be turned into a means of earning a living.

There is a great deal of help available to people starting up a business. Find out from your library, the Citizens' Advice Bureau or your professional body about grants and free advice.

This is only a very sketchy summary of the main issues. More detailed advice can be found, in the local library for example.

There is a useful book in this series, *Surviving Redundancy*, by Laurel Alexander.

CASE STUDIES

Gwen reviews her private medical insurance

It was provided by Hugh's employer before he retired, the only cost then being income tax as a fringe benefit on the premium paid by the company. However, she now has to pay the full premium and it is not only already high but increases each year well in excess of inflation as well as increasing further each time she reaches the next age bracket.

She finds out how much she would save by switching to an NHS delay policy. The existing insurer will continue to cover existing problems (she has at least one) if she switches internally.

As the saving is substantial and she sees no problem about waiting six weeks for non-emergency work, she decides to change.

Jean becomes concerned about incapacity

The family income would disappear should Alistair suffer a crippling accident or illness. His pay continues during sickness but only for a limited period.

They decide to check on the State incapacity benefit and find it would not be enough, so they look into permanent health insurance and find that the premium cost per year would be roughly equal to the benefit per month.

Jean says she could go back to full-time work if necessary but Alistair points out that he might be in a condition which requires a lot of attention and it could be too much for her.

They work out the minimum extra that they would need to live on over the State benefit and take out a policy to provide that amount.

Alistair faces redundancy problems

His old friend John telephones one evening in a panic because he has been made redundant without any warning. Alistair calms him down and offers to see him the following day (a Saturday – these things always happen on Fridays!).

Alistair thinks about the problem and when he sees John he suggests first that John reviews his finances and budgets for lower expenditure. By this time John's wife Angie has offered to go back to work as a temporary secretary, which will help a lot. Then they set about considering how to find another job. As John is over 50, it will not be easy, so Alistair suggests thinking about alternatives. Meanwhile he helps John to draft a CV.

John rings Alistair during the next week, sounding much calmer, and says he has been thinking about his hobby of visiting antique fairs, auctions and shops. Although he has never been able to spend much, he has become quite knowledgeable in certain areas – china and glass for instance. John has talked to some of the people he has got to know in the trade and they have been very encouraging.

Alistair counsels caution but agrees that it might be a good idea for John to spend some time attending auctions and buying up any bargains with a view to taking a stall at a forthcoming local antiques fair, to see whether it might be possible to earn a living, whilst still looking for a new job.

DISCUSSION POINTS

1. Do you know how much statutory sick pay you are entitled to and for how long? Does your employer go any further, either in time or amount? If not, do you need further insurance?

2. Do you know how much State redundancy pay you are currently entitled to?

3. What about long-term care? At what age (if at all) do you think insurance should be considered? Is the single premium basis a better buy, assuming you can afford it?

6

Financing Your Retirement

This chapter deals with all forms of pension, including the State basic and additional earnings-related pensions, occupational schemes and personal pensions. Help is given on such matters as the decision to retire early and the purchase of annuities.

> Remember, it is never too early to start pension planning, nor too late, and many pensions will be less than expected.

With current tax relief, for those on a marginal tax rate of 22%, a pension contribution of £100 only costs £77 (and for those on 40% it only costs £60) and then earns income and capital gains free of tax (except that tax deducted from dividends can no longer be recovered).

So pensions are a very **tax-efficient** investment. (Income tax is of course payable when the pension is received.)

A useful rough guide is that to achieve a pension of £20,000 a year from 65 a man needs to pay about £250 a month starting at age 30, £500 starting at 40 and £1,000 at 50. Women should add 10%.

MAXIMISING THE STATE PENSION

The State basic pension

The State basic pension is currently about 17% of national average earnings and as it is adjusted in line with inflation rather than average earnings (which usually increase by more than inflation), it is eroding over time as a percentage. Some say that by the year 2020 it could have fallen to only 10% of national average earnings. Consequently it is not enough on its own.

The amount received depends on **sufficient contributions** having been made. When nearing retirement age, and especially if retiring early, it is worth checking your contribution position, as additional contributions can be made to catch up on any gaps (ask your local Benefits Agency office for an application form for a retirement pension forecast).

The State basic pension is taxable. The amounts are adjusted each year and the current figures are shown in Figure 4.

The pension can be left in after normal retiring age, up to the age of 70. It increases in amount at the rate of 7.5% a year. This is not a very good deal, as (assuming average interest rates) it takes about twelve years to recover the amount sacrificed.

Just before you start receiving the State pension you should receive a statement showing your entitlement and thereafter you should receive another statement each year, showing increases.

The State additional pension (SERPS)

The State additional pension (formerly called the State earnings-related pension scheme, hence SERPS) is paid in respect of each year in which an employee's National Insurance contributions have been made in respect of earnings between the lower and upper earnings limits. These limits vary each year. It is not available to the self-employed, who do not contribute.

The amount of pension payable is a complicated calculation, which is explained in the relevant leaflet. The formula changed with effect from April 2000 and will result in gradually lower amounts over the next few years.

From April 2002 SERPS will be replaced by a new Second State Pension (SSP).

Contracting out

Many occupational pension schemes contract all members out of SERPS. The scheme must guarantee to equal the SERPS pension. In that case, lower National Insurance contributions are paid, the difference being described as a rebate.

Employees who have a personal pension scheme (see below) can also contract out providing their scheme is approved (it is then called an APP – **approved personal pension**). In this case there is no rebate. Instead the DSS make a payment to the scheme based on the NI contributions made: this must be applied for by the personal pension provider.

Investment charges for personal pensions bite hard if you contract out on a salary of less than £10,000 a year.

State basic pension

Single contributor gets £66.75 a week ⎱
Spouse – non-contributory £39.95 a week ⎰ £103.40

SERPS:
Upper earnings limit – £500 a week
Lower earnings limit – £66 a week

Age-related percentages for company money purchase schemes (and some salary-related schemes) to be paid by DSS:

Range from age 15 – 1.6% (3.1% minus employers' rebate of 1.5%) to age 47 and over – 7.5% (9.0% minus 1.5%) (the percentages vary slightly at some ages in later years)

Age-related percentages for approved personal pension schemes to be paid by DSS:

Range from age 15 – 3.4%
to age 46 – 9.0%

Fig. 4. Current State pension data.

Annual adjustments
Like the State basic pension, SERPS in payment is adjusted annually in line with inflation.

Up till 1997 there was a guaranteed minimum pension (GMP), which is also adjusted annually. In respect of pension earned up to 1988, the GMP adjustment is met entirely by the State and is added to the State basic pension. Thereafter, the scheme meets the adjustment up to 3% per annum and the State meets any further adjustment required if inflation exceeds 3%.

DSS guide NP46 gives details of SERPS (see Appendix B under 'pensions'). Current amounts are shown in Figure 4.

The State graduated pension
Before SERPS was introduced in 1975, there was another scheme called the graduated pension, which operated from 1961. There was no contracting out. The graduated pension is 7.35p per week for every £7.50 contributed by a man or £9 by a woman.

Pension forecasts

The pension forecast and the annual statement referred to above under the State basic pension will include figures (if any) for SERPS and the graduated pension.

Pensioners' minimum income guarantee

Single pensioners are guaranteed a minimum income of £82 a week (£127 for a married couple), with higher amounts for those aged 80, to be adjusted annually in line with earnings rather than price inflation.

The extra is paid as income support so recipients must be eligible for it; in particular the maximum savings amount of £12,000 applies.

JOINING AN OCCUPATIONAL PENSION SCHEME

These are schemes arranged by an employer for employees. There are two basic types – final salary and money purchase.

Final salary

In the past most company schemes have been (and many still are) final salary schemes. This means that the pension is based on the salary immediately before retirement, or the average of the last three years (sometimes the highest consecutive three in the last ten years). This is described as the **final pensionable salary** (FPS for short).

The advantage of this type of scheme is that the pension amount is known in advance with some degree of certainty. The benefits are fixed and it is the contributions which vary (in practice only the employers' contributions vary, as the employees' contribution – if any – is normally a fixed percentage of salary).

The amount of pension entitlement is calculated by multiplying the FPS by a fraction in respect of each year of service. This may be 80ths, 60ths or preferably a lower figure.

Taking 60ths as an example (it is the most common), 1/60th of FPS for each year of service means that after 30 years' service the pension would be 30/60ths or half of FPS. After 40 years' service the Inland Revenue maximum of 2/3rds (see below) would be reached.

Money purchase

The money purchase type of scheme is the direct opposite of the final salary scheme, in that the contributions are fixed and the benefits vary. Employers nervous of the unlimited commitment to final salary schemes have in recent times tended to favour money purchase, for obvious reasons.

For employees, however, the uncertainty of benefits from money purchase is a distinct disadvantage. The problem is twofold, not knowing how much the invested contributions will earn and also not knowing what pension the final lump sum will purchase because of the effect of variable interest rates on annuity rates.

Questions to ask before joining

- Is it final salary or money purchase?

- Is it contracted out of the State additional pension (SERPS)?

- What are the contribution rates, employer and employee?

- Can a tax-free lump sum be taken on retirement?

- Is there a contingent spouse's pension?

- What happens in the event of death in service or in retirement?

- What happens if employment is ended, by either party?

- What would be the effect of being laid off without pay, or short-time working?

and if it is a final salary scheme:

- How is the pension calculated?

- Is there any post-retirement adjustment to the pension for inflation and is it guaranteed or only discretionary?

- What are the rules for early or late retirement and is there any difference if early retirement is due to ill-health?

Part-time employees can no longer be excluded from membership.

Inland Revenue limits

Because of the tax-free nature of pension schemes (except of course when pensions are paid) limits are imposed by the Inland Revenue as follows:

- Maximum pension – 2/3rds of final salary (but this can include fringe benefits – company car, etc. – at the taxable amount, averaged over the three years before retirement).

- Maximum pension for spouse on death of pensioner – 2/3rds of the pensioner's pension (i.e. 4/9ths of final salary).

- Minimum service for maximum pension – 20 years (i.e. 30ths).

- Contribution limit – employee: 15% of salary.
  – employer: none.

- Post-retirement adjustment – full inflation beyond the State requirement.

- Lump sum cash – 1½ times FPS after 20 years' service, otherwise less, in proportion to service.

Hardly anyone reaches all the Inland Revenue limits.

There is also a maximum salary for new members (and all members of new schemes since 14 March 1989). It is reviewed annually in the Budget, the current amount being £91,800.

Leaving service

Only those with less than two years' service can obtain a refund of contributions on leaving and 20% is deducted for tax.

Otherwise it is a question of leaving behind a **deferred pension** (a pension payable from some date in the future, usually the normal retirement date for the scheme) or taking a transfer to another scheme (including a personal pension scheme).

Transfers

The first thing to remember regarding this question is that there is no hurry because a transfer can be obtained at any time.

The way transfers work is that the actuary of the existing scheme calculates a **transfer value**, this being the capital value of accrued benefits.

The transferer should then ask the new scheme what benefits this transfer value will buy. It is important to take account of all the benefits in the existing scheme, including any subsequent inflation-proofing. In this connection, compulsory adjustment of pensions, including deferred pensions, in proportion to inflation up to 5% per annum, was introduced for all pensions earned after April 1997.

An occupational scheme may offer additional years' service (added years) for a transfer, but usually it will be a fixed amount of pension, which is the poorer alternative as there is no protection against future inflation.

The Financial Services Authority (FSA) has issued a factsheet for people thinking of a transfer – see Appendix B.

Persons who took a transfer to a personal pension when leaving since April 1988 may have been given bad advice and are included in the review currently being undertaken as described below under opt-outs.

Points to bear in mind when considering a transfer
- The employer usually pays the administrative costs of a company scheme whereas the member pays in a personal scheme.

- Final salary is more certain than money purchase (personal pension schemes are invariably money purchase).

- The company scheme may make discretionary increases to pensions.

A company called Lexis (Tel: (01952) 463 436) for £150 will give advice on transfer to a personal pension.

Opt-outs
This term is used to describe decisions by existing employees to leave their employers' pension scheme, in favour of a personal pension. (New employees who decide not to join their employers' scheme are called non-joiners but the following comments apply to them, too.)

The FSA has issued a leaflet on the subject (see Appendix B) which recommends that in nearly every case the employer's scheme is likely to be the better choice.

Bad advice
In the past there have been some bad recommendations in respect of transfers and opt-outs from and non-joiners of employers' pension schemes in favour of personal pensions, due to unscrupulous advisers not pointing out all the advantages of the occupational scheme. Great care should be taken before deciding to transfer in this way.

The FSA has issued guidance notes on steps to be taken to review and, where appropriate, give compensation in respect of such cases and has issued a list of priority groups.

All those who were sold a personal pension between April 1988 and June 1994 should have received a questionnaire from their pension provider. The FSA are also urging occupational schemes to take members back. (See Appendix B for an FSA leaflet about this review and for information about fee-paid help on whether bad advice can be proved. Free initial legal advice is also available.)

Retirement
Final salary occupational pensions commence on retirement (whether normal, early or late) but money purchase pension schemes can now offer the right to defer purchasing an annuity up

to age 75, with income drawdown in the meantime (as with personal pensions).

Early retirement
On early retirement, pensions are lower for two reasons – **less service** and **earlier payment**. The latter effect is recognised by the application of an early retirement factor (ERF) to the calculated pension. The ERF is likely to be at least 4% for each year not worked. However, employers tend to waive it if they are encouraging early retirement. Also many schemes waive it in respect of ill-health early retirement.

A decision to retire early should not be taken lightly. Bear in mind that the State pension is not payable until later (although some employers offering early retirement may make up the temporary shortfall). Calculate how much you need to live on and add to your pension any other income. Do not forget to allow for tax.

See Figure 5 for an example of a retirement statement which involves early retirement.

Cash lump sum on retirement
Most schemes include an option to take a cash lump sum on retirement. It is pleasant to have this decision to make, but it may not be easy. Remember you can choose to take as much as you like up to the scheme limit, but you lose pension in proportion.

If a pension is inflation-proofed, then it might be better to keep the pension intact. If not, then it might be possible to buy an **annuity** (see below) with the cash which pays more after tax than the pension foregone, depending on annuity rates at the time.

You may want some cash to pay off your mortgage or at least reduce it (again it is possible to calculate and compare the alternatives). But think carefully before taking cash for a holiday or new car!

Additional voluntary contributions (AVCs)
All occupational schemes are now required to have arrangements for employee members to make additional voluntary contributions and anyone who can afford it and is not already up to Inland Revenue limits should certainly consider doing so.

The maximum employee contribution to the main scheme and AVCs together is 15% of pay. As the usual level of employee contribution to the main scheme is 5%, there is ample space for AVCs, and of course if there is no employee contribution then the full 15% is available.

ABC plc pension plan

Statement of retirement benefits for – Mr T Atkins as at 31 August 1996.

Information on which calculations have been based:

Date of birth	31.8.1934	
Normal retirement date	31.8.1999	
Pensionable service from	1.9.1977	
Pensionable salary over last 12 months		£20,000

Pre-commuted pension

£20,000 × 19/60 (note 1)	=	£6,333
Less: ERF – 3 years at 4% (note 2)	=	760
	=	5,573
Plus: AVC £15,000 ÷ 12 (note 3)	=	1,250
	=	£6,823

Cashable benefit

The maximum tax-free cash you can take at retirement amounts to:

£20,000 × 3/2 × 19/20 (note 4)	=	£28,500
The pension equivalent of this (note 3)	=	£2,375
Your annual pension would therefore reduce to	=	£4,448

Notes

1. This assumes a 60ths scheme, so the pension payable after 19 years service is 19/60ths of final pensionable salary.

2. The early retirement factor (ERF) for the scheme is assumed to be 4%, so since the pension is to be paid 3 years early it is reduced by 12%.

3. This assumes an AVC (additional voluntary contributions) fund of £15,000 has been built up. It is divided by the scheme's annuity rate at 62, assumed as 12.

4. Under Inland Revenue rules the maximum tax-free cash of 1½ times salary requires a minimum service of 20 years, so it has to be reduced proportionally for only 19 years.

Fig. 5. Specimen quotation for early retirement.

Additional benefits earned are usually on a money purchase basis, but may be in the form of additional years of service.

One disadvantage of AVCs commencing after 8 April 1987 is that you cannot take a cash lump sum on retirement.

It is possible to make AVC contributions outside the company scheme, i.e. to a **free-standing** AVC (FSAVC), which gives more freedom. However, the returns may be lower as the employer does not pay the expenses.

AVC benefits can be taken at any time between the ages of 50 and 75 (as with personal pensions) if the scheme permits, whether or not you have taken retirement from the main scheme.

AVCs versus ISAs

There is some debate about whether AVCs are better value than ISAs (for ISAs see Chapter 9 under 'tax-efficient investments'). With AVCs the contribution is tax-free but the benefit is taxable, whereas ISAs are the other way round. Both are free of income and capital gains taxes whilst the money is in the scheme. Charges might be higher for pension schemes than for ISAs.

Most experts favour AVCs because the tax gain comes at the beginning and so funds accumulate on a tax-free basis. The main advantage of ISAs is complete freedom of action, but this may not be a good thing for pension money.

This comparison is further confused by the discontinuation of tax credits for dividend income in pension schemes from 1997 and in ISAs from 2004.

AVOIDING THE PERILS OF PERSONAL PENSIONS

Personal pensions are designed for people without company schemes (or who wish to be independent of their employer), the self-employed, those who change jobs frequently and those in irregular work. The basis of all personal pensions is money purchase, so there is no guarantee of benefit level.

Most schemes are either **unit-linked** or on a **with-profit** basis. Unit-linked have the disadvantage of being tied to some extent to the stock market, which might be low when retirement time comes, although there are now ways round this (see below under 'retirement').

With-profit schemes have the advantage that bonuses, once declared, are guaranteed. However, they are less flexible and so investment performance may suffer. Unitised with-profit schemes are a combination, in that they are invested in units but bonuses are secure.

Unit-linked schemes may be invested in units in a pension fund or a unit or investment trust.

So-called **'lifestyle' investment** in personal pensions refers to flexibility of investment, where equities are used first but as retirement date approaches there is a gradual switch to fixed interest investment, to avoid the adverse impact of a sudden fall in the stock market just before having to buy an annuity.

Watch out for proposals for **'LISAs'** (lifetime individual savings accounts).

Contributions

Contributions can be paid regularly each month or, if income is irregular, whenever they can be afforded. Some people (especially self-employed) prefer to wait until the year end in order to see how much they can afford.

There is an advantage from an investment point of view of regular contributions. It is called **pound/cost averaging**, which is explained fully in Chapter 9 under 'investing in equities', but briefly means that when the stock market is low, you get more shares or units for your regular contribution than when it is high.

On the other hand, there are also advantages in making single premium payments. It means you are not committed to the one provider, so you can shop around each time and charges tend to be lower. However, you lose the discipline of having to make regular contributions.

It is sensible to start early with a relatively small payment if necessary, with the option to increase in the future, to reduce or stop if necessary and to top up at any time. So flexibility is clearly desirable.

Following the discontinuation of tax credits for dividend income in pension schemes there is a need to consider increasing your contributions to maintain your target pension.

Inland Revenue limits

Maximum contributions start at 17.5% of earnings and increase with age up to 40% for over 60s, subject to the same earnings limit as occupational schemes. From April 2001, when stakeholder pensions come in, it will be possible to make annual contributions of up to £3,600 to personal or stakeholder pensions, or both combined, the earnings-related limits only applying to higher levels of contributions.

There is no limit to the amount of pension which can be paid, and the lump-sum option on retirement is 25% of the fund.

Starting a personal pension

Shop around with a list of questions:

- What amount of pension can be expected from at least two levels of contribution? (Find out about the assumed rate of inflation.)

- How flexible can the contributions be?

- What are the charges?

- What are the penalties (if any) for stopping and/or transferring?

- What happens if you die before buying an annuity – is the fund protected from IHT?

- Are there penalties if you buy your annuity elsewhere (some providers charge 5% if they lose the business)?

- What is the past growth record (not forgetting that it is not necessarily a guide to the future)?

- How safe will your fund be?

If you decide to use an adviser to help you find a pension provider, see Appendix B for how to get a list of advisers in your area. Ask about fees.

Contracting out

Employee personal pensions can be contracted out in the same way as occupational schemes. They are then called approved personal pensions (APPs). There is no rebate, but the DSS make equivalent payments to the APP (see above under State additional pension).

Job changes

Personal pensions do of course remain with you through job changes, so there is no need to consider transfers. However, if a new job carries with it a company scheme it may be worth joining, leaving the personal pension without further contributions for the time being, or using it for AVCs or even transferring it if advantageous.

Retirement

On retirement, the funds in a personal pension scheme (except for the 25% lump-sum option) must be used to buy an annuity. However, not only may the stock market be low at the critical time, but annuity rates may also be low, due to low interest rates – potentially a double blow.

However, it is now possible to defer the purchase of some or all of the annuity up to the age of 75 and draw income directly from the pension fund whilst waiting for annuity rates to improve. This can only be done in respect of new schemes after May 1995 but existing schemes can be transferred. There are also maximum and minimum limits on how much pension can be drawn in the interim period. Income drawn this way is taxable.

Deferment can clearly be advantageous if retirement can also be phased, perhaps by doing part-time work for a year or two. The lump-sum option is not affected by deferment and funds left in continue to grow free of tax.

Advice on income drawdown can be obtained from The Income Drawdown Advisory Bureau – Tel: (020) 7401 2040.

Open market option
Most personal pension schemes include an **open market option**, which means you do not have to accept the annuity offered by the pension provider but can shop around. See below under 'annuities'.

Current criticisms
There have been many criticisms of personal pensions, particularly in the case of people who have been wrongly tempted away from company schemes by unscrupulous agents seeking commission at any price.

This has already been referred to above under 'transfers from occupational schemes'. The actions listed there are also available to people who consider they have been given bad advice without there having been a transfer from another scheme.

Pension mortgages
A personal pension and a mortgage can be combined. This has been described in detail in the section on mortgages in Chapter 4.

STARTING A STAKEHOLDER PENSION

Stakeholder pensions will be introduced in April 2001. Contribution limits are to be the same as for personal pensions.

Contributions will be made net of standard rate tax: higher rate taxpayers will get relief through their annual tax return. Retirement rules are the same as for personal pensions.

Annual charges are capped at 1% of fund value, with no initial charges and no penalties for transferring the fund or suspending contributions.

Stakeholder pensions can be held alongside existing personal pensions or company money-purchase schemes (but not final-salary schemes).

GETTING ANNUITIES RIGHT

As already explained, money purchase and personal pension funds must eventually be used to buy an annuity on retirement. This is called a **compulsory purchase annuity** (CPA) and all the receipts are taxable.

Voluntary purchase of an annuity, for example with the lump sum taken from the pension scheme on retirement, is called a **purchased life annuity** (PLA) and only the interest element of the receipts are taxable (around half of the receipts are capital repayment).

The provider of the annuity normally deducts tax at the standard rate of 22% so, if your marginal rate is less or more, you will have to claim a refund or pay extra.

For a man aged 60, the current rule-of-thumb calculation for an annuity is 8%, i.e. the annual pension will be about 8% of the funds available. Unfortunately, for a woman the percentage is less, due to longer life expectancy – 7% at 60, (but watch out for the introduction of 'unisex' annuities – the same rates for males and females). It is possible to arrange annual increases, but the starting figure will be less.

There is a wide choice of type of annuity and there can also be a wide variation in rates available, so make sure your pension provider gives you all the alternatives. Make sure though that no penalty is payable if you do go elsewhere.

Also the annuity can be investment-related, that is in a unit-linked or with-profits fund. The difference here is that the income will vary depending on performance, which may not suit many people, but it is another way of avoiding being locked in to a low income.

The Annuity Bureau Ltd will give help in buying an annuity. Tel: (020) 7620 4090 for an information pack. Annuity Direct have a guide – Tel: (020) 7375 1175.

ARRANGING DEATH BENEFITS

For any and all pension schemes you have, if there is a lump-sum death benefit it is sensible to ensure that payment is made direct to your chosen beneficiaries and so kept out of your estate and any inheritance tax liability. This can usually be done by completing a simple form from the pension provider.

PLANNING FOR YOUR RETIREMENT

Mention has already been made (under State basic pension) of the need to check, near your retirement date, your contribution position under the State scheme, to see whether any additional contributions will achieve a higher State pension.

Most occupational pension schemes will provide a quote showing your potential pension. A look at this a few years before retirement will indicate whether it might be a good idea to start or increase an AVC.

If you have a personal pension, the provider will give an estimate of the lump sum available on retirement and an indication of the amount of annuity this will buy. You can then consider additional contributions.

It is good idea to prepare a new income and expenditure budget for after retirement. This will take account of the lower levels of income and expenditure which then apply.

A year or two before retirement you should review any investments you have, with particular reference to arranging changes towards income rather than growth, should there be a need for more income. Consider whether to take action regarding any mortgage which continues into retirement.

Many employers offer pre-retirement courses and/or books or magazines. These deal with money matters and also all the other aspects of retirement, which are equally important. The Pre-Retirement Association (Tel: (01483) 301 170) run courses.

For free booklets on retirement planning contact: Kidsons Impey – *Planning for a profitable retirement*. Tel: (020) 7405 2088, or Towry Law – *How to make your money work harder and pay less tax in retirement*. Tel: (01753) 868 244.

See Appendix B for further information and advice on pensions and Appendix C for complaints.

CASE STUDIES

Floella thinks about pension mortgages

A customer of Floella's has been talking about pension mortgages, saying that they are a cheap combination. Winston says, 'Don't be daft, we need all our money now and we won't be retiring for 40 years'. However, Floella thinks that, because Winston is now at a high level of earnings (and tax rate) with the disco becoming so successful, he could be putting some money away.

They talk to an independent adviser, who recommends a flexible scheme whereby Winston can put in a lump sum of, say, £1,000 at the end of each tax year. With the tax rebate it only costs £780 – about £15 a week. He also explains that when they buy a house they can turn the pension scheme into a pension mortgage, whereby the pension cash lump sum will pay off the mortgage.

They agree to think about it for the future, when they have found a flat.

Jean's sister has a pension problem

Jean's younger sister Mary is a high-flyer but not financially wise. Three years ago she was persuaded to leave her employer's pension scheme in favour of a personal pension. She now thinks she may have been misled.

Jean has heard about this on the radio in the *Money Programme* and tells Mary that she can apply to have her case reviewed. If she has been misled then she can transfer back and possibly obtain compensation.

Mary checks with her local Citizens' Advice Bureau, who advise her to make a formal application to her pension provider in order to start the official enquiry.

Gwen's son prefers ISAs to pensions

Arthur is self-employed in computer software and is financially literate. He has worked out that the amount he can put into pensions is no more than he can invest in ISAs each year (currently £5,000). Personal pensions include high fees, whereas ISA costs are now very low.

He has worked out that, although the tax treatment varies, the final outcome is the same and ISAs are more flexible and charges lower. Gwen says can he trust himself to leave the money in for retirement, as you have to with pensions.

DISCUSSION POINTS

1. If you start a personal pension, should you contract out of the State additional pension (SERPS)? What factors should be taken into account?

2. You are in a final salary pension scheme. A financial adviser has been round to see you, painting a rosy picture if you opt out into a personal pension. He is coming back next week. What questions will you ask him? What is the most important figure you need in order to make a sensible decision?

3. You are thinking about retiring early. What information do you need to help decide? What will be the effect of taking part of the pension in the form of a cash lump sum?

7

Acquiring Basic Financial Skills

RUNNING YOUR BANK/BUILDING SOCIETY ACCOUNTS

Current accounts

Most people have a current account to handle their basic money business. Pay or pension is credited to their account, payments are made by cheque, standing order or direct debit and cash needs are met by withdrawals. Many couples have a joint account, usually on the basis of one signature only being required on cheques.

Bank cards

Cheques are supported by bank cards, whereby a payment of up to £50 or £100 is guaranteed to the payee by the bank if the card number is written on the back of the cheque.

Bank cards are also used for **cash withdrawals** from cash machines, making it possible to get cash at any time from a machine outside any branch of that bank.

Many cards are now extended to the Cirrus international cash card, which makes it possible to draw cash abroad wherever the Cirrus symbol is displayed. The UK pin number is used. The charge is 2% plus the normal exchange rate difference.

Making deposits

Cheques or cash can be paid in and you need to remember that it takes time for a cheque to **clear**, i.e. for the bank to find out that it has been accepted by the payer's bank.

Following consumer pressure, clearance time has recently been reduced to three days in most cases. It is vital to know your own bank's clearance time, if you wish to use the money from a cheque paid in as soon as possible.

Standing orders and direct debits

The difference between standing orders and direct debits is important. **Standing orders** are instructions to your bank to pay a set amount to a specified person on a set date: an example might be payment of the monthly premium on a life assurance policy.

Direct debits are instructions to your bank to pay to a specified commercial organisation any amount requested by them at any time. An example here could be a quarterly gas bill.

Whilst they are less trouble than making payments each time, the disadvantage of direct debits is the loss of control: if the other party makes a mistake it can be difficult to get it rectified because the bank will only act on the instruction of the other party.

Charges and interest

The current practice of banks is to pay a small interest rate on current accounts and not to impose charges for the services so far discussed. This situation could change in the future.

If a cheque of yours 'bounces', i.e. there are insufficient cleared funds to meet it and it is sent back to the payee's bank, your bank will make a charge. There are charges for other services, such as overdrafts (see Chapter 3 under 'managing borrowing').

Telephone banking

The success of telephone banking has led to its increasing availability. The advantage is that you can ring the bank at any time of the day or night to conduct business, access being obtained by a series of code words and questions.

Internet banking

This is the latest development. If your computer is linked to the internet, some banks have software which enables you to conduct business that way.

Opening an account

The following issues should be considered:

- Would a telephone or internet account suit you?

- Is the local branch conveniently situated?

- Is it open on Saturdays?

- Are there cash machines outside, so that you can get money when the branch is closed?

- What is the clearance time for cheques paid in?

- What interest is paid on the current account balance?

- What charges are payable – on normal transactions, on bounced cheques?

- What are the rules about overdrafts – is there a 'free' amount (i.e. no fee), what fees are payable above that, what interest rate is charged and what is the limit? (See Chapter 3 under 'managing borrowing' for overdrafts.)

Giro
The Giro system operated by Alliance and Leicester Building Society includes all the usual current account services (and there are deposit accounts too). The difference is that transactions can be carried out at **post offices**, which are open for longer hours than banks. In addition it includes both a telephone and a postal facility. Explanatory leaflets are available at post offices.

National Savings ordinary account
This is like a bank current account and is convenient for small savers. You can deposit a minimum of £10 a time. However, there are no facilities such as cheque books and standing orders.

The interest rate is low (1.25%) but is tax-free for up to £70 a year (£140 for a joint account) and a higher rate of 1.35% is payable for every complete month the balance exceeds £500. See Appendix B for source of current interest rates.

Deposits and withdrawals are made at post offices. Up to £100 can be withdrawn on demand and larger amounts within a few days.

MANAGING YOUR CREDIT AND DEBIT CARDS

Credit cards
It has become a recognised convenience to many people to have a bank or building society credit card, which can be used to settle accounts instead of cash or cheque. It saves carrying around much cash, saves writing cheques and most of all it gives between one and two months' free credit. Also if the card is used to purchase goods or services of a value in excess of £100, there is an element of consumer protection.

Most people have either Access or Visa cards. Some have both. There is a wide choice, with many different benefits. There may or may not be an annual charge.

Accounts can be on a joint basis, so that a couple can each have a card on the same account.

Limits

There will be a limit to the amount of debt you can run up on your card. You can try for the highest you can get and if it is too low, apply later for an increase, because it can be extremely inconvenient (as well as embarrassing) to be turned down in a shop because you have reached the limit. On the other hand some people prefer a low limit as a control on their spending.

Statements

The normal practice is for statements to be sent out monthly, with payment being due two or three weeks later. Longer credit is available if required, on payment of at least 10% of the total amount outstanding each month, but interest then becomes payable, at a rate usually at least 10% above base rate.

If it is intended to use the card for credit longer than the interest-free period, it is important to compare **interest rates**. This can be difficult because practice varies on what is included. Rates are expressed as the annual percentage rate (APR). However, APR does not take account of when interest starts, i.e. is it the date of the relevant payment or the date of the statement? Also there may be no free period if money is still owing from the previous month.

Always check your statements carefully as mistakes occur. If you are doubtful about interest charges, which are difficult to check, ask for a worked calculation.

Liability in event of loss

Another factor to be aware of is the extent of **liability** if the card is lost or stolen. Certainly there is a need to report the loss immediately, which can be difficult if you have a lot of cards or are abroad. It is worth spending the fee of some £8 a year to one of the organisations which will report the loss for you, following only one telephone call.

Cash

Most cards can be used to draw cash, but normally interest is charged from the date of withdrawal, so this facility should only be used in an emergency.

Foreign use

Credit cards are particularly useful on foreign holidays. Card companies usually convert to sterling at the middle rate ruling on the date of use, so there is no risk of loss (or profit) from currency fluctuation. There is usually a 1% charge, which is less than the cost of travellers cheques or foreign currency purchase.

Sensible use of a credit card

Some people do not trust themselves with a credit card, as they fear running themselves into debt. Certainly you should be aware of the implications of spending more than you can repay before interest is charged.

If you are going to make a major purchase with your card, it is worth remembering the normal date of your monthly bill as it might be worth waiting a few days to get another month's free credit.

Debit cards

These differ from credit cards in that there is no credit, no fee and no protection. When a debit card is used, the amount is debited to your bank account immediately. Two are currently available – Delta and Switch – and usually they are combined with the bank cheque card already mentioned.

A debit card is an easy way to pay and it does impose a form of self-control not available with a credit card – you can only use it if there is enough in your bank account. For those not in need of such control, the loss of free credit and of consumer protection makes the debit card less attractive.

One valuable use may be the facility to obtain cash at certain supermarkets if it is not convenient to get to your bank.

An international direct debit system called **Maestro** works in the same way, the charge being 2% in addition to the exchange rate difference, which makes it more expensive than a credit card. Maestro is a standard extension to most UK bank debit cards.

Store cards

Some stores will only accept their own credit card, so it is worth having their card, which operates in a similar way to credit cards. However, the rate of interest charged after the free period may be higher than on your credit card.

ATTACKING YOUR INCOME TAX BILL

Employees

For those in employment income tax is deducted from pay by a system known as **pay-as-you-earn** (PAYE). Each individual has a code number (notified to you in January or February for the following tax year) which is set at a figure intended to spread annual allowances (and any annual deductions) evenly over the year, so that a proportional amount of tax is deducted from each weekly or monthly pay cheque. There is an Inland Revenue (IR) leaflet on PAYE – see Appendix B.

Company directors, and employees (including pensioners) with more complex tax affairs, are required to complete **self-assessment** tax returns (see below).

Students who work in the holidays and whose total income for the year is below the personal allowance can avoid PAYE. Get form P385 from your local tax office and submit it to your employer. (National Insurance deductions cannot be avoided.)

Self-employed

There is no PAYE system for the self-employed, who must deal with their own tax affairs (or employ an accountant).

The system is well explained in IR leaflets (see Appendix B). Briefly, the self-employed person prepares accounts for a trading year (the tax people call it the **accounting year**) which does not have to coincide with the tax year (that starts on 6 April).

If you are self-employed you must submit **self-assessment** tax returns (see below).

Self-assessment

The new self-assessment system is now in full operation. If you are in the system you receive the forms in April and if you wish the tax office to calculate your liability you must submit them by 30 September. You will be notified of the **amount due**, which is to be paid half by 31 January and half by 31 July. (Employees who only have a small liability will get it added to their code number for the following year.)

If you are prepared to calculate your own liability (perhaps because you are employing an accountant to do it) you have until 31 January to submit the return but it must be accompanied by half the calculated payment.

You may be required (especially if self-employed) to make **payments**

on account in respect of the current tax year. Such amounts are notified to you if you submit your return by 30 September, or form part of the calculation if you do it yourself. These payments on account are due half on 31 January in the current tax year and half on the following 31 July.

Allowances and reliefs

Annual allowances vary in the Budget nearly every year. Some are full and some are restricted. Amounts are given in an Inland Revenue leaflet (see Appendix B) and current amounts are shown in Figure 6. The main allowances are:

- personal
- married couples (now only available where at least one partner was born before 6th April 1935)
- blind person.

Loan from employer
An employee can be given a loan of up to £5,000 at no or low interest: above that amount tax is payable on the imputed interest (i.e. at an assumed rate).

Golden handshakes
This is a payment on termination of employment. Up to £30,000 is exempt from tax, subject to meeting certain requirements.

Relocation expenses
Up to £8,000 is exempt from tax.

Private use of mobile phone
This is all tax free.

Renting a room in your house
If you receive less than £4,250 a year, it is tax-free. Above that it gets complicated – see relevant IR leaflet (Appendix B).

Maintenance payments
You may be able to get tax relief for these – see IR leaflet in Appendix B.

Pension contributions
Contributions to approved pension schemes within specified limits

are an allowable deduction from income tax liability (see Chapter 6 under occupational schemes and personal pensions).

EIS and VCTs
Contributions to enterprise investment schemes and venture capital trusts of up to £150,000 and £100,000 a year respectively are an allowable deduction from income tax at 20%.

Rates of income tax
Rates of income tax (on earnings in excess of allowances) are applied in bands which also vary year by year. Details are in an IR leaflet, see Appendix B. Current rates are shown in Figure 6.

Tax credits
These have replaced certain National Insurance benefits and are payable either through the PAYE system or directly as at present. A children's tax credit worth £8.50 per week will be introduced in April 2001.

Working families tax credit
This replaces family credit. There is a basic tax credit of £52.30 a week, with additional payments for children depending on the age of the child, a further amount if the main earner works for more than 30 hours a week, and a childcare tax credit covering 70% of childcare costs up to certain limits.

For every pound of net family income above £90 a week, 55p of credit is withdrawn, a lower withdrawal rate than under family credit.

Disabled persons' tax credit
This replaces the disability working allowance. The amount of credit is £54.30, with additional amounts for lone parents/couples, for chidlren and for those working more than 30 hours a week. The withdrawal rate will be the same as for the working families tax credit. The threshold for withdrawal will be £90 for couples, £70 for single persons.

Tax on investment income
Investment income is taxed at 20% unless total income in the year enters the 40% band. Then a further 20% is payable on any income in that band from which 20% tax has been deducted at source.

If total income for the year is below the 20% band, investment income is taxed at 10% and if it is below the 10% band it is tax free. Tax deducted at source at 20% can be recovered.

Investment income is treated as the top slice of income, so that the allowances and lower rate bands are used against earned income first.

Tax is deducted from bank and building society interest at the rate of 20% before it is paid, unless recipients have completed a form (obtainable from the bank/building society) saying that their total income is below their total allowances.

Dividends on shares are also taxed at source. From April 1999 the system changed. The imputed tax rate reduced to 10% and non-taxpayers are no longer able to recover it. For higher rate taxpayers the additional tax is at the rate of 22.5% of the gross dividend, which has the effect of leaving them in the same position as at present.

Investments can be transferred between spouses to take advantage of one having lower income tax rates than the other, without incurring capital gains or inheritance tax liabilities, or stamp duty.

Investment income not taxable

Income from the following investments is free of tax (and see Chapter 9):

- National Savings certificates and children's bonds
- TESSAs (until maturity)
- PEPs
- ISAs
- Friendly Society savings schemes.

Fringe benefits

Certain employee benefits, such as a **company car**, are taxable. The employer makes a return at the end of each year on form P11D showing the amount of taxable benefits for each relevant employee. See Figure 6 for current amount.

National Insurance contributions

These are in effect a tax on **earned income**. If you are an **employee** and your earnings exceed the lower earnings level, currently £76 a week, you pay 10% (8.4% if contracted out of SERPS) on earnings between the lower and upper earnings level, which is currently £535 a week.

If you are **self-employed** you pay on profits above the small earnings exemption, currently £3,822 a year. You pay a flat rate of £2 a week in respect of profits up to the lower profits level, currently

Allowances:

       Personal   £4,385*
       Elderly married couple £2,000*, limited to 10%
       Blind person   £1,400
       * Higher mounts if over 65 and 75, subject to income limit

Rates:

       First £1,520 is taxed at 10%
       Next £26,880 at 22%
       Above that at 40%

Employee benefits – taxable:

       Car – 0–2,500 miles pa – 35% of list price
              2,501–17,900 – reduced by one-third
              18,000 and over – reduced by two-thirds
              (all less one-third if car over 4 years old)
       Car fuel – 1,400 cc – £1,010 (petrol) £1,280 (diesel)
              – 1,401 – 2,000 – £1,280 (petrol) £1,280 (diesel)
              – over 2,000 – £1,890 (petrol) £1,890 (diesel)
       Private use of company van – under 4 years old – £500
                           – 4 years old or more – £350

Fig. 6. Current income tax data.

£4,420 a year, and 7% on profits between the lower and upper profits level, which is currently £27,820 a year.

Further details are available in leaflets from your local Contributions Agency – see your local telephone book.

Further advice

Inland Revenue leaflets are available on all matters relating to income tax and Help the Aged have an excellent leaflet – *Check Your Tax*. See Appendix B.

BENEFITING FROM SOCIAL SECURITY

The main benefits are:

Child benefit

Child benefit is payable for each child under 16 or, if in full-time education, under 19. There are no limits or deductions – every child is eligible. The amounts are changed each year – see relevant leaflet in Appendix B. The current amounts per week are £15 for the first child and £10 for each other child (£15.50 and £10.35 from 2001).

Income support
Qualifications for benefit:

- you work for fewer than 16 hours a week, but (unless a lone parent) are available for work

- your savings are less than £6,000, with proportional reductions up to £12,000.

How much you can get depends on the result of an assessment of your needs. That amount is reduced by the earnings of you and your partner above a minimum amount, which increases for each dependent child. The self-employed are allowed to deduct certain expenses from earnings before they are used to offset the benefit.

There are many factors which may be taken into account, e.g. maintenance payments.

The benefit is tax-free.

Housing benefit
Those in receipt of income support who pay rent will usually get 100% of the eligible rent. Others may also be entitled to housing benefit, particularly those in receipt of family credit. There are income and capital limits. The benefit is tax-free.

Council tax benefit
The rules are basically the same as for housing benefit, except that the maximum benefit is limited to council tax band E (up to £120,000 in value). Properties in bands F, G and H will not receive more.

Other benefits and allowances
Incapacity benefits and attendance allowance have been dealt with in Chapter 5 and retirement benefits in Chapter 6. Other benefits and allowances include industrial death or injury, maternity and widows.

In addition, many in receipt of other benefits qualify for help with NHS costs, such as prescriptions, dental and optical costs.

Leaflet FB 2, available from your local Benefits Agency office, lists all the many benefits available. Details are given of the amounts payable, any applicable 'means testing' and a brief summary of the qualifying rules. Separate leaflets for each benefit give further information.

INCREASING YOUR INCOME

Getting the minimum wage

Now that a minimum hourly rate of £3.60 (if aged over 21, £3 for those aged 18–21) has been introduced, are you getting it? If not, you can force your employer to comply.

Improving your present job

Can you earn more money by increasing your hours of work? Can you get promotion? What do you need to do to make it possible? Is it worth your while to study for an applicable qualification?

Changing your employer

Do you think you can get a better paid similar job elsewhere? If so, you ought to be applying. Look at Chapter 5 under redundancy for advice on how to set about it.

Changing your occupation

If you have an ability in another direction, which has potential for higher earnings, is it worth trying to change now? Would it be better to study to improve your skills or perhaps acquire a qualification before making the change?

Do you have a hobby which is capable of being turned into a worthwhile occupation? How about acquiring entirely new skills?

Moonlighting

If you cannot extend the hours in your present job, is it possible to take on a second job, perhaps part-time? However, you must be careful not to over-extend yourself. Your main job, which is your main source of income, must not be adversely affected. Possibly your existing employer would object.

Taking in lodgers or tenants

You can let furnished rooms, for example. Expenses can be charged against income for tax purposes but there is a risk of incurring capital gains tax on subsequent sale of the property. Income from such lettings is currently free of income tax up to £4,250 a year. See Appendix B under tax for the Inland Revenue leaflets on the tax position.

You can of course charge up more expenses if you take in a lodger whom you feed as well. See *Taking in Students* in this series.

Arranging home equity release schemes

These are schemes whereby elderly people can raise more income from their home. There are three kinds:

Home income plans

An **interest-only mortgage** is taken out and used to buy an annuity. Part of the annuity pays the loan interest. The balance is additional income. The mortgage is repaid from the proceeds of selling the home after the death of the occupant(s). To avoid uncertainty about future income, a fixed interest mortgage is desirable.

Home reversion schemes

Here part or all of the house is sold to an institutional investor for a proportion of the value (depending on the age of the seller). The buyer grants a free lease for life to the seller.

Roll-up loans

A lump sum is borrowed and you do not have to repay capital or interest before your death unless your loan plus interest outstanding exceeds, for example 75% of your house value. You therefore take on the risk of an adverse movement of interest rates causing premature repayment.

The minimum age at which they become viable is 75 (or combined ages of 160 for a couple). In all cases it is vital to take legal advice. In the past some ruthless providers have attracted bad publicity for these schemes, but they are now much more acceptable.

Remember that the income from the annuity is subject to tax only on the interest portion and only at 20%. A free leaflet is available from SHIP (Safe Home Income Plans campaign) – Tel: (020) 8390 8166. For a free fact sheet on raising income from your home, contact Age Concern on (020) 8679 8000.

REDUCING OUTGOINGS

The first thing to do is to review all expenses to see where economies can be achieved. Perhaps some luxury items can be avoided or pruned. Significant savings can be achieved in living expenses as well as luxuries by shopping around.

Can heating costs at home be reduced by improving insulation? Grants may be available – see the booklet *Home Repair Assistance* available from the Department of the Environment or your local authority.

For further ideas try the leaflet *Thinking about Money* prepared by Help The Aged but useful to anyone. It is available from the Citizens' Advice Bureau.

Budget plans

Some suppliers of goods or services offer budget plans for 'easy payment'. These are only a form of paying in advance and it is important to check that it is worth doing by working out the APR.

Sometimes no interest is offered on your advance payment, such as when buying stamps in shops as a means of saving up for Christmas. It may be more advantageous to save up in a deposit account thus earning some interest.

CASE STUDIES

Belle has benefit problems

Floella's friend Belle is a lone parent. She has a part-time job of fewer than 16 hours a week and has no savings, so is entitled to income support. Now she has the opportunity to extend her working hours to 20 a week, which she can manage as her mum will help look after the child. The longer hours take her out of income support but she becomes eligible for working families tax credit. It is all so complicated and she doesn't know what to do.

Floella suggests she goes along to the Citizens' Advice Bureau and fortunately they understand the complications and point out to Belle that as she is a single parent she will not be forced to take the additional work, so she can choose.

They explain working families tax credit and give Belle an indication of what she can expect to get, which doesn't seem so bad after all and means that it will be worth working the extra hours.

Alistair and Jean plan a foreign holiday

Alistair, ever cautious, suggests that as they have a joint credit card they take out another card and he will take one and she the other, so that if one is lost or stolen and has to be stopped the other can still be used.

They decide to take only a small amount of foreign currency – £100 – with travellers cheques to cover further requirements. They choose sterling cheques because you only pay the exchange rate difference when you use them and any left over can be used back home or kept till next time.

Gwen has difficulties with tax

Hugh did it all but now he has gone she cannot cope. Gwen's widow's pension is taxed via PAYE, but there are all the investments – building society interest and dividends. She thinks about going to an accountant but an old work colleague of Hugh comes to the rescue. He explains about tax deducted at source in some cases and at which rates, paid gross in others but taxable and finally those which are tax-free.

He offers to sort it out this year and show her how to do it in future. Fortunately he also knows about the widow's bereavement allowance, which she can claim for two years.

DISCUSSION POINTS

1. What are the advantages and disadvantages of telephone and internet banking compared with high street banking?

2. What are the most important features of a credit card in two situations – where you intend to pay in full each month and where you intend to build up a debt?

3. If you needed to increase your earnings, what would you do?

8

Becoming Your Own Investment Adviser

GRASPING THE LANGUAGE OF INVESTMENT

Fixed interest investments

Fixed interest investments are those where the income is a fixed amount, although in some cases it can change during the period of investment, such as in a bank deposit account. Usually the capital value is also fixed, although in some cases this can change, such as gilts. However, either income or capital (and in many cases both) are fixed.

The inflation/tax catch

'Real' rates of interest are the rates in excess of inflation. Usually they are in the region of 3%.

However, where interest is taxable, the inflation portion is taxable too, so high interest rates are not necessarily a good thing for taxpayers who wish to preserve the real value of their investments. See Figure 7 for the breakeven points for 22% and 40% taxpayers.

Equities

Equities are **investments** in ordinary stocks and shares in companies, where both the income and the capital value can vary up and down. They can be bought and sold on a stock exchange.

They participate in profits, after any debenture and loan stocks and preference shares, and receive dividends, usually half-yearly. Income is therefore variable.

The value of equities fluctuates with the success of the company and with the general view of the market. In other words, as financial advisers have to tell us, the value of shares can go down as well as up.

Shares have a **par** value – usually £1 or 50p – but this bears no relationship to their market value and can be ignored for all practical purposes.

Table of after-tax real rates of interest (i.e. rates after allowing for inflation), assuming a pre-tax real rate of 3%. Note the breakeven point for inflation protection, at 20% and 40%.

Rate of inflation	Total interest	Net of 20% tax		Net of 40% tax	
		Total return	Real return + or -	Total return	Real return + or -
%	%	%	%	%	%
2	5	4	+2	3	+1
4½	7½	6	+1½	4½	−
7	10	8	+ 1	6	-1
12	15	12	−	9	-3

Fig. 7. The inflation/tax catch.

Events in the life-cycle of shares

New issues

In recent times many new issues have been as the result of denationalisation, or **privatisation**, such as British Telecom and British Gas, or additional shares on de-mutualisation of building societies, but any company coming to the Stock Exchange for the first time is a new issue.

They are advertised in some newspapers. Application forms are printed in newspapers or are available on request. You fill in the form stating how many shares you want and send it off with a cheque. Following a recent change, new issues no longer have to be available to anyone.

If the issue is successful, you may not get all the shares you asked for. Some people take this into account and apply for more than they expect to get. They may be in for a quick profit, intending to sell the shares immediately – they are called **stags**.

There is no commission or stamp duty on new issues and frequently the full amount required is payable in instalments.

Rights issues

This term describes the issue by a company of further shares for cash to existing shareholders on a proportional basis (e.g. one new share for every two existing shares held).

The price is usually set below the current market price, so that the rights to take up the new shares have a market value. This is the difference between the old market price and the new issue price divided by the proportion of old shares to new – for instance, in the case of one for two, the difference would be divided by two.

Shareholders can choose whether to take up the rights by paying the price or to sell the rights. Those taking no action have the rights sold for them.

See Figure 8 for an example of how to calculate the value of rights.

Assumptions
Present market price of share – 200p
Rights issue – 1 new share for every 5 held, at 150p per share

Calculation
Excess of market price over rights price = 200 – 150 = 50p
Divide that by the number of old shares for each new one
Value of rights = 50/5 = 10p each

What will the share price be after the new issue (assuming no other change)?

5 existing shares at 200p = 1,000p
1 new share at 150p   =   150p

Total – 6 shares   1,150p = 191p per share

Fig. 8. How to calculate the value of rights.

Bonus issues
This is a misnomer – there is no bonus! The term describes the sub-division of existing shares, usually each one into two, thus doubling the number of shares and of course halving their value.

No new money passes and the action is taken usually because the market price of the individual share has risen to a level which is considered to be too high (the market seems to prefer shares to be priced below £10 each).

Scrip dividends
Sometimes companies offer shareholders the opportunity to take new shares instead of a cash dividend. This is called a **scrip dividend**. People in the top income tax bracket may prefer to do this, as a cheap way of investing more in a company they favour.

Take-over bids

From time to time one company will attempt to take over another by offering an attractive price. It is worth waiting for a competitive offer, even if the directors of the company being bid for recommend acceptance. Many newspapers will comment and speculate on what might happen.

If the buying company is successful, it can enforce the sale against reluctant sellers and is bound to accept sellers at the best price offered.

Receivership or liquidation

If a company fails and a lender of money to the company appoints a receiver or the creditors enforce liquidation, it is unlikely that the shareholders will recover much, if anything. That is the risk which ordinary shareholders run – they are at the end of the queue for return of capital.

Fixed interest versus equities

Shares can go down as well as up, but all statistics show that in the long run equities beat fixed interest investments by a substantial amount and also beat inflation, whereas fixed interest may not even achieve that (see Figure 9).

Although the yield on equities is less than fixed interest to start with, it catches up and passes it in the longer run (see Figure 10).

But to achieve the best returns on equities it is necessary to have flexibility in the timing of both buying and selling, particularly selling.

Shares carry three opportunities/risks: first the fortunes of the individual company, second that of the market sector – engineering compared with stores for example – and third the overall market movement.

A balanced portfolio

When considering any investment, whether in the form of savings or as a lump sum, it is sensible to aim at an overall balance of investments – what the experts call a **balanced portfolio**. In other words you should have a mixture of fixed interest and equity investments and a spread of investments in each category.

Risk

The more money you have invested and the longer you can leave it alone, the more risk you can afford to take with some of it. The most

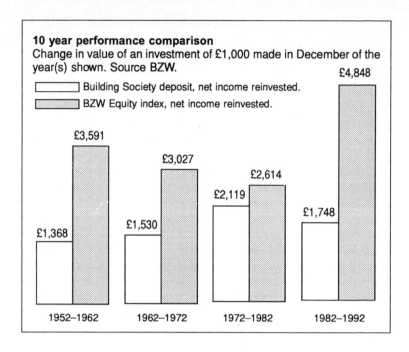

Fig. 9. Comparison of growth of fixed interest and equity.

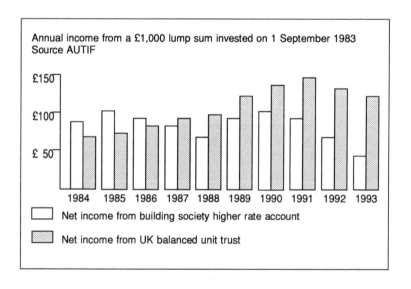

Fig. 10. Comparison of income from fixed interest and equity.

important thing is to recognise the existence of risk and to take appropriate steps.

For example, you may decide to invest directly in equities. It would not be sensible to invest it all in one company. A better strategy would be to spread it over say ten shares, which means you need to have at least £10,000 available to invest, as individual investments in shares of much less than £1,000 are not economic, due to minimum dealing charges.

> **Remember that, whilst high risks achieve high returns, the chances of loss must be equally high. You cannot expect to get it right every time.**

What we are also talking about here is **active** versus **passive** investment. A high risk strategy demands activity. Passive investing – letting others take the strain – is safer even though less exciting.

Choosing an investment category

The issues to consider are:

1. Do you want protection against inflation? Remember that in the long run equities stand a much better chance of achieving it (see Figure 9 above). Index-linked products can be considered for fixed interest investing.

2. Do you want income? Income-producing equity investments can achieve growth as well, but there is no point in investing in a product where income has to be paid out if you would rather it were left in.

3. Can you afford to take risks? An American fund manager said that investment should be boring: 'Like watching a tortoise race a hare'. Clearly his philosophy was safety first.

Questions to ask about any investment

- Capital – does it remain unchanged or can it go up and down?
- Income – is it fixed or variable?
            – is it paid out, kept in, re-invested?
- Tax – are capital gains taxable?
         – is income tax-free, taxable or taxed?

- Guarantees, of capital and/or income – are there any?

- Period of investment – is it fixed or variable?

- Risks, to capital and income – what are they?

- Commission – is any deducted and who gets it?

- Management fees – how much, if any, initial and/or annual?

- Past performance – what is it, remembering it may not be maintained?

- Future performance – what could affect it?

Warnings

- Beware of the hard sell.

- Beware of apparent bargains – if they look too good to be true, they probably are!

- Read the small print, especially where there are guarantees: find out exactly what is being guaranteed.

- Beware of fashions. They do not last and by the time you join in it may already be too late.

- Do not churn, i.e. continually buying and selling. It is expensive and fritters away the profits.

- Above all, do not panic when share prices fall. Take the long view.

Advice and complaints

Financial advisers are either **tied** to a supplier of financial products (for example, agents for Allied Dunbar or any other similar organisation), or **independent**.

Independent advisers receive their income either from commission or fees, or sometimes from both. Even when you know how much commission is being received and are prepared to pay a fee if it is inadequate, can you be sure that commission-based advice is completely unbiased? Many independent commentators suggest not.

Appendix B under 'investment' tells you how to obtain a list of independent advisers in your area and a list of fee-based advisers. How to complain is spelt out in Appendix C under 'investment'.

UNDERSTANDING HOW STOCK EXCHANGES WORK

The London Stock Exchange (LSE) is a market place for the purchase and sale of stocks and shares. Until recently it really was a market place, with a dealing floor, but now it is all electronic – you can telephone your broker to deal and will be told the current buying or selling price and if you decide to go ahead the deal will be done immediately, whilst you are on the line. You can also deal on the internet.

There are two groups participating in the market – **stockbrokers** and **market-makers**:

- Stockbrokers are agents for buyers and sellers. They arrange the deal and receive commission.

- Market-makers (formerly called jobbers) buy from you and sell to you. They receive the difference between the buying and selling price, which is called the margin, spread or 'touch'. They may also carry stocks on their books (or even a deficit in stock), thus hoping to gain from market movements in their favour.

In addition to commission, stamp duty of ½%, rounded up to the nearest £5, is payable on purchases.

SETS (Stock Exchange Electronic Trading System, also called order-driven trading) has now been introduced for FTSE 100 share deals in excess of £4,000 and it may be extended to the mid 250 shares. With this electronic system, buyers and sellers are automatically matched. Market-makers are replaced by intermediaries, who undertake to buy or sell shares where there are no matching trades.

It was hoped that the new system would reduce the spread, but unfortunately, at the beginning and again at the end of the trading day, the spread has widened and until this situation has been corrected you are advised to avoid dealing at these times.

The animals

The Stock Exchange, like many British institutions, is full of nicknames. You have already met stags, but there are two principal animals – **bulls** and **bears**. Bulls are optimistic and believe share prices will go up (a bull market). Bears take the opposite view.

To go with the meat, there are also chips! **Blue chips** are shares in companies considered to be relatively safe and sound – large reliable companies such as ICI and the big banks, usually among the 30 largest quoted companies. Then there are **white chips** – also fairly reliable, but smaller.

Share prices

Prices of popular shares are printed in most daily and evening newspapers. See Appendix B for more information on how to obtain share prices.

Share prices in the newspapers are usually grouped into sectors set by the Stock Exchange, such as stores, electrical, engineering. Tables of share prices will include some or all of the following:

- Yesterday's closing price – this being the middle market price, half-way between the buying and selling prices.

- Yesterday's increase/decrease – shown as + or – the previous day's price.

- Highest and lowest prices in the last 52 weeks.

- Market capitalisation – total number of shares times current price; a measure of company size.

- Gross yield – the last full year's dividend before tax as a percentage of the current price.

- P/E ratio – price divided by earnings (profit after tax) per share, i.e. how many years' earnings to recover the share price: theoretically the higher the figure the better potential growth, but this measure should be used with care.

In addition there may be a number of footnotes relating to individual shares.

Share price indices

Most people have heard of 'footsie'. This refers to the FT/SE (*Financial Times*/Stock Exchange) 100 Index. It is the index of the largest 100 companies by market capitalisation and the most commonly used index of UK share prices.

The other main index is the **all-share index**, which applies to all shares quoted on the LSE. There is also the **mid 250**, which covers the next 250 below the top 100.

Settlement

Settlement is now made in five working days after the transaction date and this may be reduced to three days, which may give rise to a need for payment in advance for purchases.

Most transactions are now settled electronically through the **Crest** system under which share ownership is registered in the name of a nominee. Special arrangements are necessary for the receipt of company reports and shareholders' perks, possibly at additional cost. Some brokers even charge for passing on dividends.

The old system using transfer forms and share certificates is still available but some brokers charge extra for using it.

Stockbrokers

Stockbrokers operate either on an execution-only basis, whereby they just deal in accordance with instructions (the cheapest) or they provide advice as well.

See Appendix B for how to obtain a list of execution-only brokers.

The cheapest execution-only brokers charge as little as £10 for a deal of up to £1,000 and only 1% thereafter. It is usually necessary to register with them in advance.

See Appendix C for advice on how to make complaints about stockbrokers and the availability of compensation.

INTERPRETING COMPANY REPORTS

If you invest directly in shares you should (subject to any restrictions in respect of nominee accounts) receive copies of company reports. If you are considering an investment in a company it will send you a copy of the current report (ask the company secretary). The *Financial Times* will send at no cost annual reports of companies showing a 'spades' symbol in the share price list.

Companies are required to send to shareholders an **annual report** and you will also receive an interim report showing the results of the first half year in summarised form. Some large companies send out abbreviated reports to individual shareholders who agree to accept them.

Annual report

The annual report, which includes the annual **accounts**, is usually a glossy affair which the company uses for publicity and marketing purposes. It may also be long and wordy, because parts are required by law.

To find out what really matters without having to read it all, consider the following:

Summary
At or near the beginning there is likely to be a summary of the figures, perhaps called Financial Highlights. Read that first and compare each figure with last year's equivalent. Look especially at earnings per share (EPS), as this is a most valuable statistic to the shareholder. EPS is the profit for the period divided by the number of shares in issue.

Chairman's statement
This will summarise the results, but as it is not a legal document it will be slanted favourably. The most important paragraph will probably be the last one – prospects.

Directors' report
See if there are any changes in accounting practice, which must be reported here. If there are, what is their effect on the comparisons in the summary (they should have been changed, too).

Auditors' report
Is it 'clean' – in other words have they said that anything is wrong?

Profit and loss account
The important figures are in the summary, but there will also be a useful analysis of profit between on-going business and (if any) new business and discontinued business.

Balance sheet
Look at the group balance sheet if there is more than one. Compare each figure with last year and think about any wide deviation, looking at the relevant notes. Look particularly at the net current assets and borrowings.

Cash flow statement
See whether there is a net inflow or outflow and in the latter case try to work out why, in case it is a warning sign. (Remember that a company can be highly profitable but still in trouble due to shortage of cash.)

Notes on the accounts
Read the note showing directors' pay. It is very interesting!

List of directors
This may be at the beginning or anywhere in the report. Does the company have non-executive directors and if so how powerful do they seem to be as individuals?

A guide to company annual reports can be obtained from ProShare for £4.95 – Tel: (020) 7600 0984.

Interim report
This is usually quite brief. It will show figures for the first half year compared with the same period last year and with the last full year. The figures will not have been audited and there is probably no balance sheet or cash-flow statement.

Pay attention to the first two items above – the summary and the chairman's statement, especially the comments on prospects. Watch out for any accounting changes which affect the comparisons.

MONITORING YOUR INVESTMENTS

It is essential to keep **records** of your investments – date of purchase or sale, price, quantity, value, is the very least you need.

It is also a good idea to record successive prices, where appropriate, as a result of checking periodically, so that you can spot a trend.

Another vital record is a diary of future events, so that you can readily check when your National Savings certificates expire, for example.

If you have a **computer**, there are a number of systems for keeping records and some for recording share prices and drawing graphs as aids to investment decisions.

MINIMISING CAPITAL GAINS TAX

Capital gains tax (CGT) is payable not only on the sale of stocks and shares but also on sale of a second home (or even part of the first home, if it is let or used only for business), on antiques, in fact on anything other than household goods and personal effects up to an individual limit in value of £6,000 and also private motor vehicles. There are also certain investment exemptions (see below).

There are a number of Inland Revenue leaflets on CGT – see list in Appendix B.

Calculating the taxable gain

Only gains since 31 March 1982 are taxable. The cost of any investment purchased before that date is taken as the market value on that date, which is usually shown in the company's annual report. There is a special rule to ensure that the gain (or loss) since 1982 is not greater than that for the whole period of ownership.

The cost is partly **indexed**, i.e. adjusted by the cumulative rate of inflation (RPI) between purchase and 5 April 1998. However, indexation cannot be taken beyond breakeven, that is it cannot be used to create a loss. Inland Revenue leaflet CGTI includes the table of capital gains tax indexation allowances for April 1998.

From April 1998, indexation is replaced by taper relief. It only applies to shares held for at least three complete years. The percentage of the gain chargeable reduces to 95% after the third complete year and by a further 5% for each successive year, to a minimum of 60% after ten complete years. An extra year is added to the score for non-business assets held on 17 March 1998.

More favourable taper relief applies to the sale of assets used in your business (if you have one), whether as a sole trader or as a partner, or shares in a company where you hold at least 5% of the voting rights (25% before 6 April 2000). Since that date it also applies to all shares owned in your employing company (previously only holdings in excess of 5%) and to all shares in unquoted and AIM quoted companies.

Where shares qualify as a business asset only from 6 April 2000, the eventual gain for shares owned on that date will have to be apportioned.

Capital losses can be set off against gains in the same year and after that there is an annual exemption, currently £7,200. As a result, few people pay capital gains tax.

If the net result of a year's transactions before the annual exemption is a loss, it can be carried forward to succeeding years. The annual exemption cannot be carried forward, but can be applied to the net gains for a year before any loss brought forward which, if not also used, can be carried forward to the following year.

For **chattels** with expected life of more than 50 years (e.g. antiques) the tax payable on disposal can be 5/3 of the excess over £6,000 if it is less than the normal calculation.

The method of calculating the chargeable gain was changed fundamentally in the March 1998 budget. The new method is shown in Figure 11.

New method of calculating the chargeable capital gain, introduced in the March 1998 Budget:

1. Calculate the indexed cost to 5 April 1998. (It will be worth doing these calculations in advance for all shares held on that date.)

2. Calculate the gain or loss after indexation on each sale. (Indexation cannot be used to create a loss.)

3. List all the gains for the year in ascending order of complete years held after 5 April 1998. An extra year is added to all holdings on 17 March 1998.

4. Set any losses in the current year against the individual gains, starting with those held for the least number of years (because this produces the lowest tax charge).

5. Apply taper relief as appropriate to each remaining gain (the earliest this can apply is after 5 April 2000 and then only to shares held on 17 March 1998).

6. Total the net gains for the year, after indexation and taper relief, and deduct the annual exempt amount (£7,200 in 2000), to arrive at the net chargeable gain for the year.

7. If you have any losses brought forward from the previous year, they are used to reduce the net chargeable gain, but in order to do this you have to go back to 4 above, as losses must be applied before taper relief. As in 4 above, the losses should be set against the individual gains on shares which have been held for the shortest period, to get the maximum benefit from taper relief. But in this case leave sufficient gains after taper relief to utilise the full annual exempt amount.

8. Any losses brought forward but not used are carried forward to the following year.

Partial sales
Where a partial sale of a holding takes place, the shares sold are identified in the following order:

1. Same day purchase and sale.

2. Sale within 30 days of purchase.

3. Previous purchases since 5 April 1998, the most recent first.

4. Purchases between 6 April 1982 and 5 April 1998.*

5. Purchases between 6 April 1965 and 5 April 1982.*

6. Purchases before 6 April 1965.*

*These are treated as pools, with average costs per share.

Fig. 11. The new method of calculating the chargeable capital gain.

Multiple dealings

Where there are multiple dealings in a share, such as successive purchases or rights issues taken up, then calculating the indexation is complicated.

The best way is to index the original cost up to the date of the next transaction, add the cost of that and index again to the next transaction and so on to April 1998.

These complications point to a need to keep full records of each transaction. An example of a taxable capital gains calculation is given in Figure 12.

Tax payable

The net chargeable gain for the year is taxed at 20%, or 40% of any falling into the 40% band when added to your income for the year.

CGT liability cannot be set against personal allowances.

Exemptions

Capital gains are exempt from CGT in the following cases:

- gilt-edged stock
- company debentures and loan stocks
- PEPs and ISAs
- permanent interest bearing shares
- enterprise investment schemes and venture capital trusts.

Retirement relief

Relief from CGT is given to business persons aged 50 or over disposing of the whole or part of their business, including their share in a partnership, or shares in a company where they have worked full-time as a director or manager and own at least 5% of the voting rights.

Following the introduction of taper relief, retirement relief is being phased out over five years starting in 1999/2000, in equal steps. In the current year, 100% relief is given on gains of up to £150,000 and 50% on those between £150,001 and £600,000.

Re-investment relief

Chargeable gains on disposals can be deferred indefinitely if the amounts realised are re-invested in new share issues from qualifying companies under the Enterprise Investment Scheme (see Chapter 9 under 'choosing tax-efficient investments').

Transaction record

Monthly CGTI*

17.1.95 Bought 1,000 shares at 210p each	0.114
Commision £20, stamp duty £10	
28.6.96 Bonus issue of 1 new share for each existing	
share held	0.063
4.10.97 Rights issue of 1 for 2 at 200p	0.019
11.2.98 Scrip dividend taken of 100 shares at 220p each	0.014
12.4.99 Sold 1,000 shares for 271p each	
Commission £20	

*Index numbers are taken from the monthly table of capital gains tax indexation allowances for April 1998.

Calculation – indexation relief
Original cost £2,100 + £20 + £10 = £2,130

The bonus issue is ignored as no cost is involved, but the number of shares doubles to 2,000.

Index to Oct. 97: 0.114 - 0.019 = 0.095

	£
£2,130 x 1.095	= 2,332
Add: rights issue cost 1,000 x £2	= 2,000
Indexed cost of 3,000 shares	4,332

Index to Feb. 98: 0.019 - 0.014 = 0.005

	£
£4,332 x 1.005	= 4,353
Add: scrip dividend cost 100 x £2.20	= 220
Index cost of 3,100 shares	4,573

Indexed cost to April 98*: £4,573 x 1.014 = 4,637

	£
Indexed cost of 1,000 shares = £4,637 x 1,000/3,100	= 1,495
Net sale proceeds 1,000 x £2.71 - £20	= 2,690
Taxable gain before taper relief	1,195

*April 1998 is the final month for indexation.

Calculation – taper relief

Complete years shares held after 6.4.98	= 2
Add 1 year as shares were held on 17.3.98	= 1
Total years for taper relief	3
Taper relief for 3 years = 5%	

Taxable gain reduced by 5% to £1,135

Fig. 12. Example of taxable capital gain calculation.

'Bed and breakfasting'

You can no longer sell shares one day and buy them back the next – (bed and breakfasting) to establish a capital gain to use up your annual allowance: at least 30 days must separate the sale and re-purchase. But you can of course buy back a different share. This is worth considering if unrealised gains are substantial. It is not worth doing in respect of losses brought forward as they can be carried forward to the next year.

The **disadvantage** is that costs of both selling and buying (including stamp duty) are incurred, although many brokers will forgo some or all of their commission on the second transaction. Also you lose the difference between the buying and selling price.

Those who have not used their full ISA allocation for the year (see Chapter 9) can 'bed and ISA', that is arrange for the re-purchase to be in a ISA. The re-purchase can be immediate.

Another way of still doing a bed and breakfast if you have a spouse (or anyone else you have joint funds with) is for you to sell and your spouse to buy back, which again can be immediate. However, there may be queries if you do it too often.

CASE STUDIES

Sanjay is a capitalist

Sanjay is Winston's boss at the supermarket. They get on very well. Winston calls him a capitalist because he has a number of privatisation shares – gas, electricity and the like. The shares had done very well but lately Sanjay has been grumbling a bit because some of them have suffered setbacks.

Winston tells Floella and it reminds her of a customer of hers, who was talking about diversification. Apparently most of the privatisation shares fall into the category of utilities and a wider spread of investment could be less risky.

Winston passes this on to Sanjay, who thinks he might sell some of the shares and reinvest elsewhere, perhaps in the supermarket where they work for a start.

Jean knows about stockbrokers

Jean's elder brother James, who has been successful, boasts of his investment prowess, but indicates he uses his bank for stock exchange transactions.

Jean has heard on *Woman's Hour* that there may be cheaper

stockbrokers and suggests he gets a list of execution-only brokers from APCIMS.

James scoffs a bit, but rings later to thank her, because he has found that there are cheaper alternatives. He picks out the cheapest and registers in advance with a view to trying them next time.

Gwen checks her year-end CGT position

Gwen has accumulated CGT losses of £10,000 from earlier years (from a disastrous investment in the business of a friend of Hugh!) and realised gains this year of £4,000. She has unrealised gains totalling around £10,000, the only one exceeding £1,000 being £3,000 on a successful unit trust valued at £7,000.

The realised gain will use up £4,000 of the annual exempt amount, leaving £3,100 available, which can be carried forward to next year and this year's annual exemption let go.

However, as Gwen has not used any of this year's ISA allowances totalling £7,000, she decides to 'bed and ISA' the unit trust unrealised gain, using up the rest of the annual exempt amount, leaving the earlier year's loss to be carried forward to next year.

DISCUSSION POINTS

1. The P/E ratio shows share price as a multiple of last year's earnings. Comparatively high figures are said to show a greater potential for share price growth. Why? What should an individual P/E ratio be compared with?

2. What do you consider are the three most important items of information in a company's annual report? Some people say cash flow is more important than profit – why do you think that is?

3. How do you work out the capital gain when you sell only part of an investment? How do you calculate the indexed cost when there has been more than one purchase?

9

Investing for Independence

INVESTING AS A NON-TAXPAYER

The non-taxpayer should avoid investments where the interest or dividend is paid after deducting tax and the tax cannot be recovered. Examples of such investments are **equity bonds**, which carry minimal life assurance cover in order to qualify for appropriate tax treatment, i.e. the fund (not the individual) pays standard rate tax on income and capital gains.

Tax-free investments (see next section), such as National Savings certificates and ISAs, are not necessarily advantageous to non-taxpayers; **taxable investments**, on which the tax can be avoided or at least recovered, might offer a better return. The non-taxpayer needs to look at returns on a pre-tax basis.

As already mentioned, tax is deducted from bank and building society interest at the rate of 20% before it is paid but non-taxpayers can arrange to receive it gross by completing a form (obtainable from the bank or building society) saying that their total income is below their income tax allowance.

Interest on gilts is paid gross.

The imputed tax at 10% on dividends cannot be recovered by non-taxpayers.

CHOOSING TAX-EFFICIENT INVESTMENTS

This section describes and explains all kinds of tax-efficient investments in order to help you decide which may be appropriate for you.

National Savings

National Savings are savings products provided by the government and are therefore a way for the government to borrow money directly from the public.

They are mainly longer-term investments. In every case the capital value does not change. Interest rates may be fixed or variable and the tax treatment varies, many being free of tax. In some cases interest is paid out, in others it is kept in until the termination date.

In the case of the fixed interest products, when general interest rates move significantly up or down the current issues may be closed to new entrants and new issues introduced at different interest rates. (The word 'issue' is used to describe the product currently available in each category; for example, we currently have the 53rd issue of fixed-interest savings certificates.)

There is a *National Savings Investment Guide* which helps choose between the wide range of products. This and leaflets about each one and one showing current interest rates are available at post offices.

This section only deals with tax-efficient National Savings products: the others are covered in the next section – fixed-interest investments.

Savings certificates

There are two kinds: those which pay a **fixed rate of interest** and those which are **index-linked**, i.e. pay a fixed rate above inflation as measured by the retail price index (RPI). There are also two periods of two years and five years.

In all cases the certificates must be held for the full period to obtain the full interest rate but can be cashed earlier at lower rates. Interest is not paid out.

The current interest rates are:

	2 years	5 years
fixed interest	4.75%	4.5%
index-linked	3.33%	2% (above inflation)

Interest is tax-free, so these issues are of particular interest to higher rate taxpayers.

There are limits to the amount which can be invested in the current issues (minimum £100, maximum £10,000 at present) but this does not affect holdings in earlier issues.

The general extension rate

Savings certificates can be retained beyond the five years but then become subject to what is called the general extension rate of interest (a rate which applies to all National Savings products which have passed the initial investment period).

This rate tends to be relatively low (currently it is only 2.58% for fixed interest and RPI plus ½% for index-linked), so re-investment in the current issue or elsewhere may be advisable. You can invest as much as you like in this way in addition to the limit on new investment.

Children's bonus bonds

These bonds have a higher rate of tax-free interest than Savings Certificates (currently 5.65%) but a low maximum limit. They can be bought in units of £25 for a child under 16, who can hold up to £1,000 in each issue until the age of 21. Interest is not paid out.

ISAs

An ISA is an **Individual Savings Account**, which replaced TESSAs and PEPs (see below) in April 1999.

The maximum annual investment in ISAs is £7,000 (£5,000 from 2001) and the account is guaranteed to run for a further nine years. There is no overall limit in amount or minimum or maximum time limits.

Up to £3,000 a year (£1,000 from 2001) can be invested in a **cash component** consisting of bank and building society accounts, UK unit trust money market funds, National Savings products which are not already tax-free and credit union deposits.

Up to £1,000 a year can be invested in **life assurance**, e.g. a with-profits bond.

The other component is **stocks and shares**, including ordinary shares, fixed interest preference and convertible shares and corporate and convertible bonds, gilts which have at least five years to maturity when bought, unit trusts, oeics (see Glossary), investment trusts, and industrial and provident societies. There are no geographical limits. There is no annual limit for this component apart from the annual total.

There are mini-ISAs and maxi-ISAs. So each year you can have one mini-ISA for each component, or one maxi-ISA. Only one manager for each is permitted each year. If you have a stocks and shares mini-ISA, the maximum investment is £3,000, so if you want to invest, say, £3,000 in the cash component and all the balance of £4,000 in stocks and shares, you must have a maxi-ISA.

Certain standards for ISAs have been introduced, called CATs (Charges, Access and Terms), to protect inexperienced savers. ISA products do not have to meet these standards, but only those which do will carry the 'CAT' mark. See Figure 13 for details.

ISAs are free of income and capital gains taxes and dividends receive a tax credit of 10% till 2004.

CAT standard for cash ISA

Charges   No charges of any kind (except for replacement documents).

Access   Minimum transaction size no greater than £10. Withdrawals within 7 working days.

Terms   Interest rate no lower than 2% below bank base rate. Upward interest rates to follow base rate changes within a calendar month (downward may be slower). No other conditions (such as a limit on frequency of withdrawals).

CAT standard for insurance ISA

Charges   Annual charge no more than 3% of fund value. No other charges (such as for the guarantee on surrender value).

Access   Minimum premium no more than £250 lump sum a year or £25 a month.

Terms   Surrender values to reflect the value of the underlying investments. After 3 years, surrender values should at least return the premiums.

CAT standard for stocks and shares ISA

Charges   Annual charge no more than 1% of net asset value (including any additional charge for ISA wrapper). No other charges.   •

Access   Minimum saving no more than £500 lump sum a year or £50 a month.

Terms   (For pooled funds such as unit trusts, oiecs and investment trusts:) Fund at least 50% invested in EU listed securities. Units and shares to be single priced at mid-market price. Investment risk to be highlighted in literature. (Plus, for investment trusts:) Gearing must not exceed 10% of net asset value. Split funds are not permitted.

Common requirements for all ISAs

Commitment to decent straightforward treatment of customers.
No bundling (i.e. requirement to buy another linked product).
Undertaking to keep to the CAT standards after the product is sold.

Fig. 13. CAT standards for ISAs.

TESSAs taken out before 6 April 1999 will run to maturity and thereafter the capital element can be transferred into the cash component of an ISA without counting against the annual limit. Some providers have TESSA-only ISAs for this purpose. The advantage of a cash ISA over a TESSA is that you can withdraw cash at any time without losing the accumulated tax-free interest.

No more PEP contributions were able to be made after 5 April 1999 but existing PEPs can be retained. A PEP investment can be transferred into an ISA (perhaps to take advantage of the wider investment opportunities) but will count against the current year's ISA allowance.

Charges in the stocks and shares component

Usually there is an **initial charge**, which may be as high as 5%, but there is a growing tendency for providers to have an **exit charge** instead, which usually reduces over time, perhaps to nil after five years. In addition there will be an **annual charge** for administering the plan, usually 1 to 1.5% of the market value.

Some large companies administer their own company ISAs and usually their charges are lower. Also some intermediaries rebate part of their commission, which saves some of the initial charge.

High yielding fixed interest ISAs may have the charges deducted from capital in order to maximise the apparent income. It is most important to recognise this when choosing an ISA.

Are they good value?

There has been some debate about the value of PEPs, particularly for standard rate taxpayers, since not many people pay capital gains tax. However, this dates back to the time when PEPs could only be invested in equities. The same questions arise in connection with investments in the new ISAs.

Now that company fixed interest stocks and shares can be invested in PEPs and ISAs, producing more income than equities at least to start with (as well as incurring less risk), there will be a tendency, particularly for higher rate taxpayers, to use PEPs and ISAs in this way.

See Figure 14 for a table showing the return required to recover annual charges.

Statistics of returns over a period are currently only available for the time when PEPs were limited to equities. They show that equity investment through a PEP achieved a higher return although it took a lengthy period for the difference to be significant. See Figure 15.

| Annual | Yield needed by taxpayer | |
charge %	20%	40%
0.50	2.95	1.47
0.75	4.41	2.20
1.00	5.88	2.94
1.25	7.34	3.67
1.50	8.81	4.40
1.75	10.28	5.14
2.00	11.75	5.88

Notes

- The tax saving for 22% taxpayers is only 20%.

- Provision is made for 17.5% VAT on the annual charge.

- No provision is made for any initial or exit charges, or any charges for receiving annual reports, etc.

- Higher returns are required by 22% taxpayers if invested in shares, as tax rebate on shares is now only 10%.

Fig. 14. Relationship of PEP and ISA charges to tax savings.

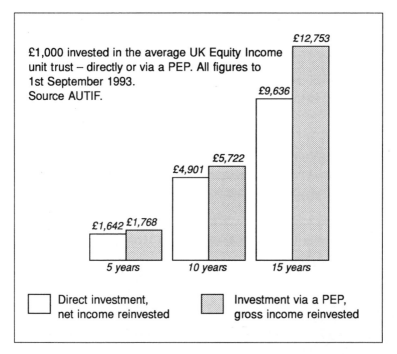

Fig. 15. The added benefits of a PEP over direct investment in unit trusts.

Choosing an ISA

Even when you have decided on the type of ISA you wish to invest in, there is still a wide choice. Here are some questions to ask the provider:

- What are the initial/exit and annual charges and are they charged to income or capital?

- What are the dealing costs (if applicable)?

- Is there a charge for transfer to another provider?

- Are there charges for switching between the provider's funds?

- Are there charges for collecting dividends, getting company reports and attending AGMs?

Further information

There is a great deal of information on ISAs, mostly from investment or unit trust providers. Usually you can choose which trusts to invest in from among those made available by the provider.

The Association of Investment Trusts (AITC) has a guide on investment trust ISAs. Hargreaves Lansdown publish a more general guide at a cost of £3 (but they might let you have it free!). There is an Inland Revenue leaflet – IR89. See Appendix B under 'ISAs' and 'tax' respectively for how to obtain any of these.

TESSAs

A TESSA is a **tax-exempt special savings account** provided by a bank or building society. It is the interest which is exempt from income tax, making this a valuable investment for taxpayers. You can only have one TESSA at a time and must be aged at least 18.

New TESSAs will not be permitted after 5 April 1999, but existing ones will run to maturity and thereafter the capital element can be transferred into the cash component of an ISA.

The maximum investment was £3,000 for the first year and £1,800 a year thereafter up to a maximum of £9,000. The money has to be left in for five years from commencement to get the tax exemption, although it is possible to take monthly payments of the non-tax-free element of the interest, i.e. less 20%.

It is possible to cancel the contract and withdraw the full amount (but not part) within the five years but the tax exemption is entirely lost. It is also possible to transfer from one provider to another, although the provider may impose penalties.

There is an Inland Revenue leaflet on TESSAs; see Appendix B under 'tax'.

PEPs

PEPs are **personal equity plans**. All income and capital gains within a PEP are free of tax and there is no minimum or maximum time limit.

Following the commencement of ISAs (see above) in April 1999 no new PEPs can be taken out but existing PEPs can be retained. From 6 April 1999 PEPs will receive a 10% tax credit on dividends till 5 April 2004.

A general PEP can be invested in a number of investments whereas a single-company PEP, as its name implies, can only be put into one company.

Qualifying investments

Qualifying investments are European Union companies' ordinary shares, investment and unit trusts which have at least 50% in qualifying investments and, for general PEPs only, UK companies' bonds including Eurobonds, European Union companies' redeemable preference shares and convertibles.

Corporate bonds and convertibles must have a maturity date five years or more after investment date. They, and preference shares, must be denominated in sterling.

Up to £1,500 in a general PEP can be in invested in a non-qualifying investment trust or unit trust, i.e. one that has less than 50% in qualifying investments, provided at least 50% of the non-qualifying portion is invested through a recognised stock exchange. Direct PEP investment in non-qualifying stocks and shares, such as gilts or non-EU companies, is not permitted.

Investments in a PEP can be changed, the only limitation being that in a single-company PEP the proceeds of a sale must be re-invested within 42 days. In other words there is no limit to the time that money in a general PEP can be left on deposit in cash form, providing there is an intention to invest.

Friendly society savings schemes

A friendly society is a **mutual insurance and savings** organisation operating for the benefit of its members. Usually it has arrangements for sickness and death benefits, as well as other forms of insurance and investment.

Friendly societies are authorised to offer a form of tax-free equity savings linked to life assurance. The maximum investment is £25 a month or £270 a year and the schemes run for a minimum of ten years.

Once in the scheme, the contributions earn income and capital gains free of tax and after ten years no tax is payable on withdrawal. There are penalties for early withdrawal. Because the amounts involved are small, some schemes have relatively high charges, which can cancel out the tax advantage.

Most providers offer schemes for children and this seems quite a good way of achieving equity investment for a child, although most children are in a tax-free position anyway, so other alternatives should be considered – see Chapter 10 under 'helping your family'.

Enterprise investment schemes and venture capital trusts

Investments for at least five years (three years for shares issued after 6 April 2000) in a new **qualifying enterprise investment scheme** (EIS) of up to £150,000 a year or **venture capital trust** (VCT) of up to £100,000 a year receive tax relief at the rate currently of 20%. Capital gains are tax free and, in the case of VCTs, so are dividends.

Arrangements can be made to defer capital gains tax on any investments realised to provide the funds for investing in new shares in this way. Losses on disposal after five years can be set against income or capital gains tax.

These are risky investments and as the tax relief is not high they are really only for the very rich who can afford to take risks with some of their wealth.

Employee-owned shares

These are now treated as business assets for capital gains tax purposes and so benefit from the four-year taper relief (see Chapter 8).

Employee share option schemes

Under these schemes the employing company grants the employee an option to buy shares in the company at some date in the future at a price based on the current share price.

Hopefully the share price will increase during the intervening period, so that when the option can be exercised a profit is made. However, if the reverse is the case nothing is lost, as the option does not have to be exercised.

If the scheme is one permitted by the Inland Revenue, no income tax (or National Insurance contributions) are payable except on any dividends paid on the shares after the option has been exercised.

Capital gains tax is payable only if and when the shares are subsequently sold (not when the option is exercised). Shares arising from the first three types of schemes shown below can be transferred to an ISA within 90 days of exercising the option.

The following schemes are accepted by the Inland Revenue:

Savings-related schemes (sometimes called Sharesave schemes)
These are linked to a **save-as-you-earn** contract (SAYE) and the total option value is limited to the maximum SAYE contract value, i.e. up to £250 a month plus the bonus after three years of three months' contributions or after five years of nine months' contributions. These schemes must be open to all employees.

The way it works is that at the commencement of the contract the employee starts an SAYE scheme with a bank or building society chosen by the employer and at the same time is offered an option to buy shares in three or five years' time at a price which can be up to 20% below the current market price.

Clearly if the shares go up in value over the period a profit is made. If the value of the shares has gone down, all is not lost as the option does not have to be exercised and the SAYE savings scheme bonuses are similar to Savings Certificates.

The bonus received at the end of the SAYE contract is tax-free. Contributions then cease (although you can start again) but in the case of the five-year contract, if the money is left in for a further two years a further bonus of nine months' contributions is received.

The bonuses are equivalent to 4.8% per annum after three years, 4.6% per annum after five years and 4.5% after seven.

CGT is calculated on the gain over the option price but taper relief starts from when the option is exercised.

All employee share schemes
This new type of scheme begins later this year. There are three sections:

- **free shares** – employees can be given up to £3,000 of shares free of tax and NICs.

- **partnership shares** – employees can be allowed to buy shares out of pre-tax income up to an annual maximum of £1,500.

- **matching shares** – employers can match partnership shares by giving employees up to two free shares for each one bought.

Free and matching shares must remain in the scheme for at least three years; partnership shares can be taken out at any time. Income tax and NICs are payable on the initial value of the shares unless they are left in for five years.

CGT is payable only on the increase in value after the shares are taken out of the scheme.

Dividends paid on the shares will be tax free if used to buy more shares.

Profit-sharing schemes

Companies can allocate a **proportion of profits** to the acquisition of shares in the company for the benefit of eligible employees. All employees with over five years' service must be eligible. The maximum value per employee in any tax year is £3,000 or 10% of salary, whichever is the greater, subject to a maximum of £8,000.

The shares must be held by trustees for at least two years. Once the shares are transferred to employees they can be sold but the proceeds are subject to income tax on a reducing basis if sold within three years of the original allocation. Thereafter they are only subject to capital gains tax.

Dividends are taxed in the normal way, whether the shares are held by the trustee or by the employee.

Schemes must be merged into an all-employee scheme after April 2002.

Company schemes (formerly executive schemes)

Unlike SAYE and profit-sharing schemes, **company schemes** may be selective in membership.

The tax reliefs for the old executive share option schemes were withdrawn on 17 July 1995 but options offered before that date and taken up are still eligible. Instead a new company scheme has been introduced, which is similar to the executive scheme except for the insertion of an upper limit to the market value of shares when options are taken up, of £30,000.

There is a three-year minimum period before options can be exercised. There may also be a requirement for minimum productivity improvement before exercise of options is permitted. Discounts are not allowed in this case – options must be offered at the full current market price.

Cash will be required to buy the shares when the option is exercised, but usually there is an arrangement with a stockbroker for immediate sale of some at least of the shares to raise all or part of the cash, with a temporary loan to cover the period between sale and receipt of the proceeds.

Enterprise management incentives
This further new scheme beginning later this year is for key people in smaller companies, i.e. independent trading companies with gross assets not exceeding £15 million.

Up to 15 employees can each be granted options on up to £100,000 of shares. In addition to the usual tax reliefs, any capital gains tax liability will be reduced by the more generous business assets taper relief (see Chapter 8), which will be counted from when the options are granted.

Premium bonds

Premium bonds are the only gamble where you do not lose your stake! Prizes are based on a tax-free return currently of 4%. The average return is less than this but much more can of course be won. On the other hand, with only a few bonds you can go on for years without winning any prize.

The minimum purchase is £100 and the maximum holding is very high. The top monthly prize is £1 million. Every investor should consider putting a small proportion of their total portfolio into premium bonds.

Investing savings in tax-efficient investments

As the minimum investment in **National Savings** certificates is £100, a holding can be built up regularly by buying a further certificate as soon as you have another £100 available.

ISAs can be used as a savings vehicle. Most unit trust ISAs will have savings schemes and cash can be accumulated in a self-select ISA until there is sufficient to invest and will earn interest tax-free by being placed on deposit by the ISA provider.

Friendly society savings schemes and SAYE share option schemes are obviously appropriate for savings.

Premium bonds can be bought £100 at a time.

MAKING FIXED-INTEREST INVESTMENTS

Fixed-interest investments are explained in Chapter 8 under the heading 'grasping the language of investment'.

Tax-free National Savings and ISAs are covered in the previous section and bank/building society deposit accounts and National Savings investment accounts in Chapter 3 under 'accumulating an emergency fund'. This section outlines other fixed-interest investments.

Term deposits

This expression is used to describe bank or building society deposits for longer periods – one to five years. Interest rates can be fixed or variable.

When interest rates are high, fixed rates are more attractive and vice versa. Naturally the providers publicise fixed rate accounts more when interest rates are low.

National Savings

National Savings have been described in general in the previous section. Taxable National Savings products are now covered.

Pensioners' bonds

These are only available to those over the age of 60. A higher rate of interest is payable than on savings certificates (currently 6%) but it is taxable (i.e. paid gross but subject to tax), so this issue is of more interest to the non-taxpayer.

The interest rate on the current issue is guaranteed for five years. Interest is paid monthly. At present the minimum investment is £500 and maximum £1 million in total.

Capital can be withdrawn before the five years is up, but two months' notice is required and no interest is paid for that period. Alternatively immediate withdrawal can be made subject to loss of 90 days' interest. Also the money can only be withdrawn after the five years if requested within two weeks of the anniversary date: otherwise another five-year period starts.

A new two-year pensioner's bond has been introduced paying 6.2%.

Capital bonds

Like many National Savings products, these earn a guaranteed rate of return over five years, this time at a higher rate (currently 6.15%) which is taxable. There is a minimum contribution of £100 and a high maximum of £250,000. They can be cashed in early, but less interest is payable.

Interest is added to the bond annually and is not paid out until repayment of the bond. An annual statement of interest is sent for tax purposes.

These may be of interest to the higher-rate taxpayer who already has the full allowance of savings certificates and doesn't need regular income.

Income bonds

These are similar to capital bonds but the interest is paid out monthly. Consequently they are more suitable than capital bonds for those who require a regular income. However, interest is variable (currently 6% for amounts up to £25,000, 6.25% for higher amounts) and is taxable.

Three months' notice is required for withdrawals. Alternatively immediate withdrawal can be made subject to loss of 90 days' interest. The minimum investment is £500 and the maximum £250,000.

Fixed rate savings bonds

Introduced in 1999 (and replacing First Option bonds for new investment) these bonds earn a fixed rate of interest over set periods of time – 6, 12 and 18 months and 3 years. Rates are tiered so the more you invest the higher the rate.

Interest can be left in or drawn out monthly or annually. There is a penalty for cashing in early. The minimum investment is £500 and the maximum £1 million.

Interest rates currently vary from 5.85% for 6 months for amounts up to £20,000 to 6.65% for 3 years for amounts over £50,000.

Gilts

British Government fixed interest stocks are described as **gilt-edged** (gilts for short) because they are considered to be supremely safe (at one time the certificates did have a gold edge). The two important facts about any gilt stock are the **interest rate** and the **redemption (repayment) date**.

The interest rate is based on the face value (the issue value) of the stock and is usually set at the market rate when the stock is issued. The percentage rate on the face value is called the coupon.

In most cases the interest is fixed but there are some which are index-linked, i.e. expressed as a fixed percentage above the retail price index (capital values of these are also index-linked).

Redemption is usually set between two dates a few years apart, leaving the government some choice. The face value is repaid on redemption. (There are a few old issues which are irredeemable; they are described as undated stocks.)

Market price

This fluctuates in accordance with the relationship between current market interest rates and the set rate on the stock. However, the length of time to redemption also influences the market price, bringing it nearer to the face value as the redemption date approaches.

Another important factor affecting price movement of gilts is that short-term interest rates tend to be more volatile than longer-term rates.

Yield

Return, or yield, on gilts is calculated on the current market price and is expressed in two ways – interest only and redemption: the latter taking into account the difference between current market price and redemption value, allowing for the time to redemption.

Interest payments

Interest is paid half-yearly and is taxable. (Capital gains are not taxable.)

Buying and selling gilts

Gilts are traded on the Stock Exchange and form by far the largest value of dealings there. However, there is another way for small investors to buy and sell – through the Bank of England Brokerage Service. Most gilts are included in it (but not all).

Purchases and sales are made by completing and posting a form, which can be obtained at any post office together with an explanatory leaflet, which lists the available stocks. The cost of dealing is 0.7% on the first £5,000 in value and 0.375% on the rest, with a minimum of £12.50 for buying only.

Dealing this way is slower and you cannot set limits and so is slightly more risky, but prices would only change significantly if there were to be a substantial change (or expected change) in interest rates.

Interest is paid gross, although in the case of purchases through the Stock Exchange, you can elect to have tax deducted at source.

Choosing a gilt

Your tax position is important. A higher rate income taxpayer may choose a gilt with a low coupon rate, because most of the redemption yield will be capital gain and so not taxable. On the other hand, a non-taxpayer would choose a high coupon gilt above par value because of the relatively high interest yield.

Basic rate taxpayers are usually recommended to avoid gilts with a current market price above par, because the capital loss to maturity will not be fully offset by the taxed income.

Bonds

The term **bond** has in the past been the generic term for fixed interest stocks with security (the borrower is 'bound' to pay interest). Gilts are therefore bonds. However, in recent times it has also been used in the name of some equity-based investments: for example, guaranteed equity bonds issued by insurance companies. Those are dealt with in the next section.

Some building societies issue bonds and some of these have interest rates which escalate, say in annual steps of 1% from 4% to 8%. The capital value is fixed.

Another building society product is called a **permanent interest-bearing share** (PIBS for short). As the name implies, there is no redemption. The interest rate is higher than for gilts and the market price moves with interest rates. PIBS can be a good investment for a fairly safe high return when interest rates are expected to fall.

Company fixed-interest investments

Debentures and loan stock

Debentures are company fixed interest stocks which are secured on some or all of the assets of the company. **Loan stock** is used to describe unsecured company fixed interest stocks. In both cases there will be a redemption date when the loan will be paid back at a stated price.

Like gilts, the rate of interest is fixed and the market price will vary. Interest on loans is payable whether or not there are profits and takes preference over any dividends. Interest rates are usually quoted gross.

Also like gilts, capital gains are tax-free.

Preference shares

These are shares in the company rather than loans to it. A fixed dividend is payable out of profits, usually before any dividend on the ordinary shares (hence the preference). Market price will vary in accordance with the market rate of interest. Dividend rates are usually quoted net of tax.

Convertibles

Convertibles are bonds or shares issued by companies, earning fixed interest or dividends, which are subsequently convertible to equity, i.e. ordinary shares. Conversion can take place after a specified date at a set price which is usually in excess of the ordinary share price when the convertibles are issued.

Investing savings in fixed-interest investments

The simplest way is to make regular payments into a bank or building society deposit account or the National Savings investment account.

The use of National Savings certificates and ISAs as savings vehicles has been covered in the previous section.

INVESTING IN EQUITIES

Investing in ISAs, friendly society savings schemes, enterprise investment schemes and venture capital trusts has been dealt with in the second section of this chapter, on tax-efficient investments. This section covers other equity investments.

Investment trusts

These are companies whose business is the buying, holding and selling of shares. In other words they make the investment decisions for you. Shares in investment trusts can be bought and sold on The Stock Exchange and dividends are paid.

There are many investment trust shares available and some invest generally while others specialise, either in general income or growth shares or in particular sectors, countries or world regions.

The share price is usually at a discount to the market value of the underlying investments (called the **net asset value** or NAV) and the amount of discount varies from time to time as well as between individual companies at any one time. In recent times discounts have been as high as 10% and as low as 2%.

Another feature of investment trusts is **gearing** – their ability to borrow money to invest, thus gearing up the opportunity for growth and/or income increase (and of course the risk of loss).

Information about investment trusts can be obtained from the Association of Investment Trusts (AITC) – see Appendix B. See Appendix C for making complaints.

Unit trusts

This is another form of pooled investment like an investment trust, but the constitution is quite different. It is a pool of funds managed by a professional company but owned separately by a trust. The price or value of a unit is the total value of the underlying investments divided by the number of units.

Units are bought and sold at varying prices, like shares, the margin being the margin of the underlying investments plus any initial charge, which may be as high as 5%.

Some unit trusts do not have an initial charge but instead have an exit charge, which may be stepped down over a period of years, perhaps to nothing after five years. From time to time initial charges may be temporarily reduced (like having a sale!). Also some advisers may rebate part of their commission, thus reducing the initial charge: they are called discount unit trust brokers.

In addition there is an annual charge in the form of a management fee, usually of around 1–2% of the value.

Unit trusts have the same variety of general and specialised investments as investment trusts.

Further information on unit trusts can be obtained from the Association of Unit Trusts (AUTIF) – see Appendix B. See Appendix C for making complaints.

Unit trusts are a singularly British institution and some are converting to the continental style open-ended investment companies (oeics), which have only one price for buying and selling and charges are separate. As they are companies, the 'units' are in fact shares. However, there is a proposal that single pricing should become compulsory for unit trusts in 2001.

Investment trusts versus unit trusts

One fundamental difference between the two is that a unit trust is **open-ended**, which means that new investors add to the total sum invested, whereas an investment trust is **close-ended**, the sum invested not changing during the life of the trust. This engenders greater volatility for the investment trust.

The opportunity for gearing and the variable discount also make investment trusts potentially more volatile than unit trusts. On the other hand, the charges for unit trusts have in the past been considered high.

Investment trusts have more autonomy of choice of when to invest and can invest in a wider range of assets, i.e. including commodities and unquoted companies. They must pay out 85% of income.

Direct investment in equities

As stated in Chapter 8, direct investment in equities should be made in a number of shares, in order to spread the risk. A portfolio of ten shares is a sensible minimum. Since an individual investment of less than, say, £1,000 is uneconomic, the minimum amount to consider investing directly is around £10,000.

When to buy and sell

We all wish we knew! Many newspaper City pages will recommend individual shares to buy or sell and this pushes the price up or down respectively, usually before you can react.

Theorists say to buy when the market starts to go up and sell when it starts down, but few of us can distinguish a blip from a trend. However, it is not a good idea to buy after a long trend upwards, as an adverse reaction is likely (and of course in reverse for selling). Another useful piece of advice is to cut losses but let profits run.

There is a great tendency to sell a share which has fallen in price (particularly when it falls below the purchase price) and to buy more of one which has risen. However, the decision should be based not on what has already happened but on what you think will happen in the future.

Nevertheless, it is sensible to set a **stop-loss price** for each share held. Experts suggest 20% below the purchase price but that figure needs to allow for general market movement. Use stop-loss not as a signal to sell but as a signal to review: the decision to hold or sell must be based on expectations for the future.

Guaranteed equity investments

There are a number of guaranteed equity investments on the market. They are offered by banks, building societies and insurance companies and are frequently described as **bonds**, e.g. guaranteed income or guaranteed growth bonds.

There is a tie-in period, usually at least five years, and a minimum investment amount, either as a lump sum or monthly saving, often both.

The **guarantee** needs careful reading. It may be for income but in the small print there may be a provision for income to be paid from capital if there is insufficient income received, especially in the case of a 'high-income' bond.

A guarantee of growth might be tied to stock-market performance, with a fall-back position of at least getting your original investment back.

An example of a growth guarantee is a minimum of 30% growth over five years, but records show that the average annual return (growth plus income) over all recent five-year periods is about 15% and there is only a 1 in 78 chance of five-year growth falling below 30%. So the guarantee might not be worth much in reality.

These products in effect offer participation in the stock market at reduced risk, which you may find suits you, but it is essential to read the small print to understand exactly what is being guaranteed.

With-profits bonds

These are lump-sum investments in the with-profits funds of life assurance companies, which invest in a mixture of equities, fixed interest and property. Annual bonuses are declared and there is usually a terminal bonus after a set period, usually at least five years, with penalties for cashing in earlier.

Returns are smoothed, thus reducing risk, but there is no guaranteed return. Bonus rates are net of basic rate income tax; higher-rate taxpayers may have to pay extra but withdrawals of up to 5% a year can be taken free of immediate higher-rate tax.

Some funds set off charges against the annual bonus, others do not, so it is necessary to take this into account when comparing. Advisers get commission – try to get a rebate.

Most bonds give the company a right to make a market value adjustment (a reduction in the amount paid out), if a bond is encashed at a time when markets are low, in order to protect the remaining investors.

Index tracking

It is possible to invest in products which are linked to an index, usually the FT/SE 100 or the all-share index.

Perfect linking cannot normally be achieved, because no fund can invest in every share in an index in the right proportions. Also the indices take no account of the costs of buying and selling, which can depress the fund compared with the index.

Some investment trusts offer **index loan stocks** which are directly linked to the relevant index and so do achieve perfect linking. They usually have a set repayment date and pay dividends. As they are unsecured there is a slight risk of a failure to repay, but they take preference over the shares in the investment trust.

Investment clubs

These are organisations which arrange cooperative investing of savings. Funds are built up by regular contributions and club members meet regularly to review their existing portfolio and select further investments, which are made by the club on behalf of the members. The disadvantage is that you have to go along with the decisions, whether you like them or not.

The Association of Investment Clubs will provide details of any club·in your area and tell you how to start one. Information can be obtained by ringing ProShare (Tel: (020) 7600 0984).

Shareholders' perks

Some companies offer perks to shareholders, usually in the form of a discount on goods or services they supply. There is usually a minimum shareholding below which the perk is not available. Experts warn not to invest merely to get the perk: the share should be worth buying for its intrinsic value.

A guide (priced £3 but possibly free) can be obtained from Hargreaves Lansdown (see Appendix B under PEPs) or from Barclays Stockbrokers (Tel: 0345 777 100).

Investing savings in equities

Investment trusts and unit trusts will have **savings plans**. As already indicated, ISAs and friendly society schemes can also be drip-fed.

The advantage of regular savings invested in equities is something called **pound/cost averaging** – a curious description of the fact that when the stock market is low, you get more shares or units for your monthly contribution than when it is high, so that the average price paid per share or unit is lower than the average of the prices paid each time you invest.

This can have a significant effect over a long period, particularly in the case of more volatile investments.

CASE STUDIES

Floella plans the wedding

Floella and Winston are putting their savings into a building society current account, where tax is deducted at source. Floella wonders whether they would be better off avoiding tax.

When she looks into it she finds that all the tax-efficient investments are for a longer term than is appropriate, as she (at least) intends the wedding to be next year!

Alistair and Jean are going to start saving

Like Floella, they also consider tax-efficient areas. The best for fixed interest would be a cash mini ISA but the saving is long term and therefore equity ISAs would be an alternative worth considering.

Alistair is nervous about the risk, but Jean points out the plus factors – statistics showing that equities have always won in the long term against both fixed interest and inflation, together with the advantage of pound/cost averaging. Alistair is not convinced, but agrees.

Gwen reviews her investments

Gwen has investments totalling £100,000. She has a TESSA (£9,000) and a building society account of £10,000, which she is building up to £12,000. She also has National Savings certificates maturing later this year totalling £10,000 and two £6,000 equity PEPs bought in previous years. The balance is invested directly in equities and unit trusts.

Gwen thinks she has too high a proportion in fixed interest and plans to increase her equity holding when the NS certificates mature, so she decides to re-invest £5,000 in equities in maxi-ISAs over the next two years.

DISCUSSION POINTS

1. What are the relative advantages of tax-free National Savings certificates to the non-taxpayer, the standard-rate payer and the higher-rate payer?

2. What are the relative merits of maxi- and mini-ISAs?

3. Scrip dividends are where you take new shares instead of a cash dividend. What are the advantages and disadvantages? Why is it a cheap way of adding to your investment? Would you rather have the income? What happens about tax?

10

Helping Others

HELPING YOUR FAMILY

Investing for children

It is possible for children to have savings in National Savings (there is a special account for children, see Chapter 9 under 'tax-efficient investments'), bank and building society accounts and investment trust and unit trust accounts. Below the age of seven, they cannot operate these accounts themselves, but someone (usually a parent) can act for them.

Children are entitled to the personal tax allowances. However, if the parents have provided the capital, then income over £100 a year for each parent is treated as theirs and taxed accordingly. This opens the door for grandparents and other relations to provide the capital. Inland Revenue form R85 can be submitted to arrange for interest to be paid gross where appropriate.

Because investing for children is frequently of a long-term nature, equity investment is highly appropriate and if payments are made regularly the pound/cost averaging rule applies (see Chapter 9 at the end of the section 'investing in equities'). Tax deducted at source on dividends can no longer be recovered. Capital gains are taxed independently.

Children under 18 cannot sign documents of title, so the usual basis is for an adult to act as **bare trustee**, shares being registered in the name of the adult with the addition of the child's initials.

See Appendix B under investment trusts and unit trusts for leaflets from the AITC and AUTIF (the latter contains a useful general guide) and under National Savings for the leaflet on children's bonus bonds.

Paying for school fees

If you want to pay for the private education of your children or grandchildren, the earlier you start to save the better. There are no tax incentives, so it is purely an investment decision as to where to save the money.

Investment

The objective is to create income of a specified annual amount (plus inflation) for specified years ahead. If the requirement is still some years away, then equity growth investments are appropriate. The AITC (see Appendix B under 'investment trusts' for obtaining their leaflet) recommend income investment trusts but unit trusts are equally suitable.

Take account of each child separately and do not commit your investment to a particular school.

Another way of paying school fees is by taking out a special form of **mortgage** which has a draw-down facility (the money is released as required). Halifax is one bank which offers this facility. Unsecured loans are also available – contact the School Fees Insurance Agency (Tel: (01628) 634291).

It is worth getting independent financial advice (see Appendix B) and there are specialists in this area. Similar considerations apply to any parental contribution to university grants (see below).

Gifted children

Help is available for gifted children, in the form of grants from charitable trusts. For further information look in your local library for *The Directory of Grant Making Trusts* or *The Education Grants Directory* for charities which make grants.

Financing further education

This is in a transitional stage, with fees being phased in, grants being phased out and loans being increased. Existing students in 1998/9 continue under the old system of grants and loans, with no fees, until the end of their course. New students from 1998/9 have to pay fees of up to £1,000 (means-tested like grants), get no grants from 1999/2000 onwards and much higher loans, with an easier loan repayment scheme (see below).

The current average annual amount needed by students is about £5,000. It will be more if the place of study is in London.

Grants

The present levels can be found in the Department for Education and Employment (DfEE) booklet which can be obtained from your county council.

If the student has income above a certain level, then a contribution is required. If the student is under 25 and is single, or married for less than two years, a parental contribution may be required. If the student has been married for two years or more, a spouse contribution may be required. Parents should consider saving for their contribution – see school fees above.

Loans
The amounts are shown in the DfEE booklet referred to above. No interest is payable, but the repayment amount is adjusted for inflation. For existing students in 1998/9 repayment is required over the five years starting in the April after the course ends (seven years in the case of a course lasting five years or more). There are various concessions, such as postponement of repayment if earnings are below 85% of the national average earnings (currently £16,488).

For new students from 1998/9, loans are paid back by instalments linked to income, the annual repayment being 9% of income above the threshold of £10,000 a year.

It is certainly worthwhile for students to take their maximum loans and invest if not used, as it should be possible to beat inflation without taking much risk.

Loans are obtained from your local education authority. Telephone 0800 405 010 for help. For further information on grants and loans see a National Union of Students information sheet – telephone (020) 7272 8900 for a copy.

Banks
Banks and building societies have free offers for students (because of the potential for getting a customer for life). This may for example include a limited amount of free overdraft.

Also available from banks are **career development loans**. The government pays the interest whilst studies are in progress but not after, although there is six months' grace if you are then unemployed. Information can be obtained from the Department for Education and Employment by telephoning 0800 585 505.

Barclays Bank has a students' guide including a money planner. Other banks produce similar literature. There is a book – *Pay Your Way as a Student* (price £7.99).

Gifts during your lifetime
These are potentially subject to inheritance tax (IHT). However, there a number of exemptions:

* Transfers between husband and wife.

- £3,000 payment from capital. (This is an annual exemption which can be carried forward for one year but not longer.)

- Small gifts – up to £250 each, unlimited in number.

- A series of regular gifts from surplus income, with no reduction in capital nor in the standard of living of the donor. (The taxpayer must be able to show that these requirements are met.)

- Gifts relating to a marriage, of up to £5,000 from a parent, £2,500 to a direct descendant (e.g. a grandchild) and £1,000 to anyone else.

- Gifts for maintenance of the family. This applies to spouse, children (up to age 18 or until completion of full-time education) and dependent relatives.

Potentially exempt transfers (PETs)
These are gifts to individuals or certain trusts which are not otherwise exempt. If the donor lives for seven years after the gift is made, no inheritance tax is payable but if the donor dies within the seven years then the PET is included in the estate for inheritance tax purposes. Term life assurance can be taken out to cover the potential IHT.

Where some of your estate is potentially subject to IHT but is largely tied up in property, a home equity release scheme (see chapter 7 under 'increasing your income') can be used to realise some or all of the amount above the threshold, to give away as a PET. However, the percentage of the home value sacrificed must be less than the IHT rate, also taking into account any sacrifice of future growth, to make it worthwhile.

Immediately chargeable transfers (ICTs)
This term applies to gifts to discretionary trusts or to companies which are not otherwise exempt. In such cases tax is immediately payable at half rate, i.e. 20%, on any amount exceeding the exempt amount (see below) on a cumulative basis with any other ICTs within the last seven years.

If death occurs within the next seven years then the ICT is included in the estate and further tax may be payable. Tax paid in this way cannot subsequently be recovered.

Taper relief
When PETs and ICTs within seven years of death are included in the estate, they are first set against the threshold in chronological order. If their total exceeds the threshold but the period since the excess amounts were paid is more than three years, taper relief applies. Tax on those amounts is reduced to 80% of the full charge (i.e. 32%) in the fourth year, 60% in the fifth year and so on.

In the case of ICTs, tax already paid is deducted from any further liability, but not so as to create a refund.

Minimising inheritance tax when you die
Benjamin Franklin said, 'Nothing in this world can be said to be certain except death and taxes'. Inheritance tax cunningly brings the two together.

On the other hand, some experts describe it as a voluntary tax, because there are so many ways of avoiding it – but they are not all straightforward.

Certainly it should be avoided if possible, as the tax rate is a swingeing 40% and it is applicable to all non-exempt gifts during the seven years before death, on a cumulative basis.

Exemptions
The first £234,000 of an estate is exempt (it is called the **exempt amount**, or threshold, and may be adjusted each year in the Budget). It may sound a lot until you think about the value of your house, if you own one.

Transfers between husband and wife are exempt but there is an advantage in finding a way of utilising some at least of the exempt amount on the first death in order to avoid or reduce any liability on the second (see under IHT planning below).

The previous section of this chapter referred to a number of gifts exempt from IHT and some of these can be made to anyone. Gifts to charities are also exempt, up to any amount, as are investments held for at least two years in any non-quoted securities and this includes investments in the alternative investment market (AIM) which meet certain criteria.

Finally there is reference in the previous section to potentially exempt transfers and immediately chargeable transfers, which again apply to all gifts.

Inheritance tax planning
The main problem for most married couples with combined assets in

excess of the threshold (including their home) is that they need their assets (especially their home) to live on during their lifetime, so they cannot afford to give any of it away.

For most married couples who have children but would normally leave everything to each other, the first consideration must be to find a way of utilising the exempt amount on the first death. There are a number of ways of doing this.

The following routes require inclusion in the will and do not come into operation until the first death:

- *The family home*
If this is owned jointly, then it passes to the survivor without forming part of the estate. However, if it is owned as **tenants-in-common** (each spouse owns half), then half will form part of the estate and part or all of that half can be willed to the children.

A further advantage of half-ownership by the family after the first death is that if the survivor has to go into long-term care, half the value of the home is excluded from the means test (see Chapter 5).

Arrangements can be made for the survivor to prevent sale of the house during his or her lifetime, but careful legal drafting is required in order to avoid the arrangement being a **gift with reservation**, which means it would stay in the estate of the survivor.

Arrangements can also be made for ownership to revert to the joint basis, which may be a better protection for the survivor. However, on either basis the children have the right to joint occupation, so disputes can arise. Consequently this course of action needs careful consideration and many experts advise against it.

- *Trusts*
There are a number of different forms of trusts which can be set up to receive a capital sum from your estate within the IHT threshold. The right one for you depends on whether the surviving spouse needs income from the capital amount or at least access to it in case of need. One form of trust loans the money or assets back to the surviving spouse, to use as he or she likes, the loan being repayable on the second death, with interest

The following are outside the will and take effect immediately:

- *Loan for investment*
This device only gives away the growth content of capital. A trust is set up and loans are made to it within the threshold, which are invested.

Up to 5% of the loan can be repaid each year, thus providing income. There is currently some doubt about whether the annual repayments are free of tax – this point needs sorting out before setting up such a trust.

- *Back-to-back plan*

An **annuity** is purchased, part of the income being used to buy life assurance to pass the capital to the children and part to provide income. It is only appropriate for those over 70, because below that age the returns on annuities are inadequate.

- *Split-capital investment trust*

This is an investment where there are **income shares** and **capital shares**. The idea is that you invest half your money in each, keep the income shares (effectively giving you the same income as before) and pass the capital shares (with the future growth) to your children up to the threshold.

All the above routes require the help of a **solicitor**, to ensure that IHT is avoided. You might consider the loan trust to be the first choice, because it has the minimum effect on the surviving spouse.

Many investment advisers offer forms of investment which fall into one or other of the trusts outlined above. Usually they require investment of all the sums involved in one place, thus earning the adviser substantial commission. But it may not be at all convenient to produce the cash, as existing investments will have to be sold. Also there is more risk from having only one investment vehicle. It is not necessary to take such action to avoid the tax.

Which? sell a *Guide to Giving and Inheriting*, price £9.99. Tel: 0800 252 100.

Lifetime gifts

For those who can afford to part with their capital and income before their death (or the death of their spouse) then more direct action can be taken either now or at death. Obviously each partner can will to the children assets up to the threshold.

Lifetime gifts can be made of **appreciating assets**. A trust can be used to benefit grandchildren as well or even to skip a generation, if that is appropriate. With the seven-year rule, such gifts can be repeated every seven years.

Yet another way is to take out life assurance, with the beneficiaries named as recipients of the benefit. This is called being 'written into trust' and most life assurance companies will provide the necessary documentation, although some make a charge. This can also be done with with-profit bonds; if held jointly, the trust can be set up to come into operation on the second death.

If you have a pension scheme which pays a lump sum if you die, ensure that it goes directly to your beneficiaries, thus bypassing your estate and any IHT liability.

Paying IHT

The problem with IHT payable on death is that it must be paid before probate is granted, but without probate the executors of the estate may not be able to get hold of the cash, so may have to borrow. (**Probate** is official permission to executors to act on the terms of a will. In the absence of a will it is necessary to take out letters of administration – the same problem arises.)

If the estate includes property, then the proportion of IHT payable equal to the proportion of the property to the total estate can be deferred.

Banks and building societies may release sums on deposit sufficient to pay for funeral expenses, cost of probate and possibly IHT.

The only other way is to prepare in advance by taking out a life assurance policy to the value of the expected IHT. The policy should be written in trust in favour of the executors.

Reducing-balance term life assurance (under which the benefit reduces with the elapse of time) is worth considering in the case of PETs.

See Appendix B for the Inland Revenue booklets on IHT. Many financial advisers offer guides: they are usually seeking business, but their literature does contain useful suggestions.

Making a will

Everyone should consider making a will and certainly those with any significant assets (including home owners) should do so, no matter how young. Where there is no will, the **intestacy rules** apply (rules for sharing out an estate in the absence of a will – see Benefits Agency booklet D49) and they may well be inappropriate for you.

It is not necessary to use a solicitor, but if there are any complications one should be considered. A free guide to making a will can be obtained from: Royal Institute for the Blind, Freepost, Bristol BS38 7AW, and *Which?* have a will pack for £10.99. Tel: 0800 252 100.

It is important to remember that a married couple can die at the same time (such as in a car accident). Provision should be made for this event by including what is called a **'survivorship' clause** so that any gifts from one to the other only apply if the other survives the first death by, say, 30 days.

It is not generally known that a will can be amended after death, provided of course that all the beneficiaries agree: this is called a **deed of variation** and requires a solicitor to draft it.

In addition to making a will, there is something to be said for leaving an explanation of it and also a set of instructions, ranging from whether you wish to be buried or cremated to where you have kept your building society passbook, etc.

Enduring powers of attorney

If you are elderly you should consider making an enduring power of attorney in favour of your spouse and children, or whoever you choose to look after your affairs if you should become incapable of doing so yourself. This document only comes into operation if you become incapable and merely has to be registered and a fee paid at that stage. It avoids the extra difficulty, expense and delay for your spouse and children in taking out a power of attorney, should it become necessary.

SUPPORTING CHARITIES

There are a number of ways of making tax-free donations to charities. It is no longer necessary to enter into a four-year covenant in order to obtain tax relief – a one-off payment of any amount now qualifies.

Supporting the gift-aid scheme

In this case a single gift is made. The payment is accompanied by Inland Revenue form R190(SD), which can be obtained from the charity or the Inland Revenue. The charity recovers 22% tax. Higher-rate taxpayers can recover the extra 18%. There is no limit to the amount of individual or total payments.

The Charities Aid Foundation (CAF)

Although covenants are no longer required, the CAF system continues to be a convenient way of making individual donations. Contributions can be paid monthly or quarterly, by standing order, and are credited to your account with the CAF, which is like a bank account. The CAF recover the tax and credit that to your account.

You are provided with a cheque book with which to make donations to registered charities and you can even use the system to pay annual membership fees to charitable bodies such as the National Trust or RSPB. The CAF have now introduced a charity card, which is a debit card, to make it even easier to make payments.

To pay for their expenses and to support the work of their founder, the National Council for Voluntary Organisations, the CAF make a deduction of 5% from contributions.

The CAF have an explanatory leaflet – Tel: (01732) 520 055.

Payroll giving
Under this arrangement an employer sets up a scheme for employees to choose to make charitable donations of an unlimited amount tax-free, either to charities of the employee's choice or (more likely) only one charity. The scheme can also be operated by a pension scheme. In addition, for the next three years, the government will add 10p to every pound donated via the scheme.

Gifts of shares
You can also give shares to a charity or to the CAF. The full market value of the shares is treated as the value for tax purposes, so you can recover 22% and higher-rate taxpayers can recover the extra 18%. In addition there is no liability for tax on any accumulated capital gains.

If you have some small parcels of shares which are not worth selling because of the effect of minimum commission, you can give them to Sharegift, which sells them in economic batches, giving the proceeds to charity (Tel: (020) 7461 4501).

Making gifts in your will
Any gift to charity by will is free of inheritance tax and a gift of assets is also free of capital gains tax on any accumulated gain. Experts suggest having a fall-back position in your will leaving all your wealth to a charity thus avoiding giving money to the State if somehow all your other bequests go wrong.

The **tax** position on all charitable donations is explained in several Inland Revenue leaflets, see Appendix B under 'tax'.

INVESTING ETHICALLY

The terms **ethical** and **green investments** are used to describe investments in companies which demonstrate that they respect the environment and/or ethical issues.

There are investment and unit trusts and ISAs specialising in ethical investing as well as specialist advisers and stockbrokers. EIRIS (Tel: 0845 606 0324) will provide free lists of ethical investments and managers and relevant independent financial advisers.

A free guide can be obtained from The Ethical Investment Association, c/o Ethical Investment Services, 33 Ribblesdale Place, Preston PR1 3NA.

The disadvantage of such funds is that they may not perform as well as funds which are less restrictive.

CASE STUDIES

Hugh and Gwen minimised inheritance tax
Hugh and Gwen's house less mortgage was worth about £270,000, investments were valued at £100,000 and other assets about £30,000, making a total of about £400,000, nearly twice the exempt allowance.

As they wanted to minimise IHT they had to do something about the house, which they jointly owned. They decided to write the simple letter, one to the other, turning their ownership into tenants-in-common, which gave them more freedom of action.

Having consulted a solicitor, they each left his/her half of the house to a family trust and now Gwen shares ownership with the trust. Now she is thinking of moving, the trust will have to agree to the sale of the house and purchase of a flat. As there will be a surplus from the transaction, Gwen and the trust will also have to decide what to do with it.

Alistair and Jean made a covenant to their church
The church had an adviser helping to raise funds. She proposed that regular attenders should enter into covenants for the annual amount of their weekly contributions, so that the church can recover the tax.

Alistair and Jean agreed to do this and realised that the covenant must be entered into by Alistair, as he is the taxpayer.

Now that covenants are no longer required, the covenant will not be renewed but records of contributions will still need to be made to permit the church to recover the tax.

Gwen goes 'green'!

Gwen reads in a wildlife magazine that there are companies which are recognised as complying with environmental standards and decides that some at least of her future investments will be in these companies. She knows that Hugh would have been sceptical and would have pointed out the risk of inadequate performance, but she gets hold of a list of ethical investments and picks out some that look good anyway.

DISCUSSION POINTS

1. Have you got some surplus income which could be funnelled into a savings scheme for your children or grandchildren? If so, what do you consider to be the best investment?

2. If you wish to make payments to charity, which method would you choose? What is the main advantage of the Charities Aid Foundation scheme?

3. If as a shareholder you consider that a company has been unethical in some way, what would you do? Write a letter to the chairman? Go along to the annual general meeting and raise the issue? Just sell the shares? Which action might have the most impact?

Appendix A
General Reading, Listening and Viewing

BOOKS

Beginner's Guide to Investment, Bernard Gray (Century Business, £12.99).

Investing in Stocks and Shares, John White (How To Books, third edition, £9.99).

A Guide to PEPs and Stock Market Investment, John Campbell (Arrow Business Books, 1994 edition, £6.99).

Allied Dunbar Investment and Savings Guide (Annual, £17.99).

Savings Guide for Older People (Age Concern, £4.95).

Which? Guide to Pensions (£9.99).

Which? Guide to Active Retirement (£12.99).

Which? Guide to Giving & Inheriting (£9.99).

Which? Way to Save & Invest (£14.99).

Unit Trust Yearbook (should be in a library).

An Introduction to Annual Reports and Accounts (ICA/ProShare). £1.25 by post from Report & Accounts, PO Box 1, Hastings TN35 4SE.

NEWSPAPERS AND MAGAZINES

Investors Chronicle (weekly, good supplements).

Moneywise (monthly).

What Investment (monthly).

Money Observer (monthly).

Financial Times (daily; Saturday editions have more price details than other days and there are quarterly supplements).

Other newspapers – *Sunday Times* has personal finance section.

Which? (monthly; has good financial section and separate annual tax guide).

RADIO

Money Box: Radio 4, Saturdays at 12 noon to 12.25 pm.
Money Box Live: Radio 4, Mondays, 3 pm to 3.30 pm.

TELEVISION

Occasional programmes on money matters:
Pound for Pound: BBC 2.
Your Money or Your Life: BBC 2.
Serious money: Channel 5.

Consumer programmes which sometimes include money matters:
The Money Programme: BBC2, Sunday evenings.
Watchdog: BBC1, Thursdays 7 pm to 7.30 pm.
Other money and consumer programmes on any channel.
Note: days and times can change.

Ceefax and Teletext: share prices, currencies and much more investment information, including some selling of investments on Teletext.

INTERNET

If you have a connection to the internet you have a further area of information available. All the main providers of investment products have web-sites and in addition there are discussion groups on personal finance matters which you can join.

Appendix B
How to Get Further Information and Advice

Note: These days almost all the organisations listed below have websites. If you have a connection to the internet you should be able to find the site using a search engine and the relevant name – e.g. Benefits Agency.

BENEFITS

You need to approach your local office – see the telephone book under Benefits Agency. They will post leaflets to you.

Useful leaflets:

CAT1	Catalogue of leaflets
CSA2084	*Child support agency*
D49	*What to do after a death*
FC1	*Family credit claims*
GL17	*Help with council tax*
GL23	*Benefit rates*
IB202	*Incapacity benefit*
IS20	*Guide to income support*
JSAL 5	*Jobseekers allowance*
SD1	*Sick or Disabled*
WK1	*Financial help if you work or are looking for work*

DEBT

For help, contact your local Citizens' Advice Bureau – see telephone book. They will post booklets to you.

Booklets available:
*Credit-wise – a guide to trouble-free credit**

Dealing with your debts
Debt – a survival guide*
Money-fax – a guide to credit and debit*
No credit? Dealing with wrong credit references*

*Supplied by the Office of Fair Trading.

Other contacts are: National Debtline ((0121) 359 8501) who will give support, advice and a self-help pack. Consumer Credit Counselling Service (CCCS), who offer free help – Tel: 0800 138 1111.

ENDOWMENTS

Beale Dobie ((01621) 85 11 33) offers information on how to buy or sell an immature policy.

The Association of Policy Market Makers ((020) 7739 3949) will provide a list of market makers in second-hand policies. Policy· Portfolio ((020) 8343 4567) have a free guide to second-hand endowment policies.

INSURANCE

Consider using an insurance broker, but remember he is a middleman and earns commission from the insurer.

Leaflets on all types of insurance can be obtained from: The Association of British Insurers, 51 Gresham Street, London EC2V 7HQ. Tel: (020) 7600 3333.

Accident & injury claims
The Law Society offers half an hour of free legal advice. Phone Accident Line free 0500 19 29 39.

INVESTMENT ADVICE

Useful guides can be obtained from:
Help the Aged 0800 650 065: *Managing a Lump Sum.*
Towry Law (0345) 88 99 33 *Guide to Retirement Planning.*
UK Debt Management Office (020) 7862 6501 *Investing in Gilts.*

For a list of independent financial advisers (IFAs) in your area, phone IFA Promotions on (0117) 971 1177. For a list of fee-based IFAs phone Money Management Register on (0117) 976 9444.

Chase de Vere's Moneyline (0800 526 091) provides lists of best interest rates.

INVESTMENT TRUSTS

Information can be obtained from AITC (Association of Investment Trust Companies), Durrant House, 8–13 Chiswell Street, London EC1Y 4YY. Tel: (020) 7431 5222.

MORTGAGES

Best buys – see *Moneyfacts* magazine. Tel: (01603) 476 747 for one free issue.

The British Bankers' Association ((020) 7216 8800) has a free guide to bank mortgages.

Endowments – to check on adequacy for mortgage repayment, see above under endowments.

ISA mortgages – fact sheet available from AUTIF – see below under unit trusts.

Tax relief – see IR123 below under tax.

NATIONAL SAVINGS

Leaflets about each product and a separate leaflet showing current interest rates are available in post offices. Current interest rates can be found on Ceefax on Channel 2 under Savings.

PENSIONS

The Occupational Pensions Advisory Service (OPAS) offers free advice regarding occupational or personal pensions. You need to write (after taking the matter as far as you can with the pension provider) to: 11 Belgrave Road, London SW1V 1RB. Tel: (020) 7233 8080.

A list of advisers offering fee-based advice on pensions can be obtained from Money Management Register – Tel: (0117) 976 9444.

Factsheets on opting out and transferring out of an employers pension scheme and on the pension transfer and opt-out review can be obtained by sending an sae to: HMSO/FSA Distributors, Sovereign Press, PO Box 10971, London SE17 3ZG.

The Registry of Pension Schemes will help trace pension rights from a previous employer. Contact **OPRA** (Occupational Pensions Regulatory Authority), PO Box 1NN, Newcastle on Tyne NE99 1NN. Tel: (0191) 225 6316.

A number of leaflets are available from the National Association of Pension Funds (NAPF) – Tel: (020) 7730 0585.

Scottish Amicable has a free booklet – a guide to real pensions. Tel: (0141) 248 2323.

The Benefits Agency has a number of booklets:

PM1 *Don't leave your pension to chance*
PM2 *You and state pensions*
PM3 *You and occupational pensions*
PM4 *You and personal pensions*
PM5 *Pensions for the self-employed*
PM6 *Pensions for women*
PM7 *Understanding contracted-out pensions*

See under Benefits (above) for obtaining these.

The Inland Revenue has IR 78 – *Personal pensions, a guide for tax* (see under Tax (below) for obtaining this).

SHARE PRICES

Most newspapers carry some share prices. The Saturday *Financial Times* has the most complete list of the week.

For price movements during the day, see Ceefax or Teletext, although their listings are somewhat limited.

There are telephone systems, e.g. Cityline ((020) 7873 4378 for a leaflet) but this can be expensive.

STOCKBROKERS

APCIMS (The Association of Private Client Investment Managers & Stockbrokers) ((020) 7247 7080) will send a list of stockbrokers showing some information about each.

TAX AND NATIONAL INSURANCE CONTRIBUTIONS

Help the Aged has a leaflet *Check your tax*. Tel: 0800 650 065 for a copy.

Various financial advisers produce guides to inheritance tax: usually they are trying to sell a relevant product, but you do not have to buy!

For Inland Revenue and Contributions Agency leaflets and for advice, contact your local tax office – see telephone book. They will post leaflets to you. You can get a catalogue of leaflets. Useful leaflets:

GT1	*Capital gains tax: an introduction*
CWL1	*Starting your own business*
IR34	*PAYE – (explains how it works)*
IR41	*Income tax and the unemployed*
IR56/NI39	*Employed or self-employed? Guide for tax and national insurance.*
IR65	*Giving to charity*
IR87	*Letting and your home*
IR89	*PEPs*
IR90 (& insert)	*Tax allowances and reliefs*
IR92	*Guide for one-parent families*
IR93	*Separation, divorce and maintenance payments*
IR95	*Profit-sharing schemes*
IR97	*SAYE share option schemes*
IR101	*Company share option plans*
IR110	*Guide for people with savings*
IR113	*Gift Aid*
IR120	*You and the Inland Revenue – standard of service*
IR123	*Mortgage interest relief*
IR133	*Income tax and company cars*
ISA/1	*The answers to ISAs*
SA/BK1	*Self-assessment – general guide*
SA/BK2	*Self-assessment – guide for self-employed*

For booklets on IHT contact the Capital Taxes Office. Tel: (0115) 974 2400.

UNIT TRUSTS

Information can be obtained from AUTIF (Association of Unit Trusts and Investment Funds), 65 Kingsway, London WC2B 6TD. Tel: (020) 7831 0898.

Appendix C
How to Complain

BANKS AND BUILDING SOCIETIES

First complain to your own branch. Then take it to the head office. Finally, write to the appropriate ombudsman:

The Banking Ombudsman, 70 Grays Inn Road, London WC1X 8NB. Tel: (0345) 660 902.

The Building Society Ombudsman, Millbank Tower, London SW1P 4QP. Tel : (020) 7931 0044.

BENEFITS

First ask your office to review their decision. If not satisfied, appeal to the relevant tribunal. Finally, approach the Social Security Commissioner.

For further information see the following leaflets:

NI246 *How to appeal*
NI260 *Guide to reviews and appeals.*

ESTATE AGENTS

Write to the head office first. Then if the agent is a member of OEA, write to:

Ombudsman for Estate Agents, Beckett House, 4 Bridge Street, Salisbury, Wilts SP1 2LZ. Tel: (01722) 333 306.

or, if a member:

National Association of Estate Agents, Arbon House, 21 Jury Street, Warwick CY34 4EH. Tel: (01926) 496 800.

Royal Institution of Chartered Surveyors, 12 Great George Street, Parliament Square, London SW1P 3AD. Tel: (020) 7222 7000.

Institution of Surveyors and Valuers, 3 Cadogan Gate, London SW1X 0AS. Tel: (020) 7235 2282.

or, if not a member of any of these, the local Office of Fair Trading (see under unfair trading).

INSURANCE

Insurance companies are self-regulated by PIA or FSA (see below under investment). The insurance company decides which.

After going to the top in the insurance company without success, refer first to: The Insurance Ombudsman, 135 Park Street, London SE1 9EA. Tel: 0845 600 6666.

Insurance brokers are regulated by a council, which in turn is governed by the FSA. After going to the top without success, write to: The Insurance Brokers Registration Council, Higham Business Centre, Midland Road, Higham Ferrers, Northants NN10 8DW. Tel: (01933) 359 083.

INVESTMENT

Complain to your adviser first.

The overall authority is the FSA (Financial Services Authority), which supervises and will be taking over several self-regulatory bodies, i.e. IMRO, PIA, SFA (see below). If in doubt as to which one applies, contact FSA Central Register ((020) 7929 3652) and they will tell you. The FSA address is:

25 The North Colonnade, Canary Wharf, London E14 5HS. Tel: (020) 7676 1000.

There is an investors compensation scheme if a regulated business goes under – the first £30,000 lost plus 90% of the next £20,000 is covered.

Investment managers and advisers are covered by IMRO (Investment Managers Regulatory Organisation), which has an Investment Ombudsman:

6 Fredericks Place, London EC2R 8BT. Tel: (020) 7796 3065.

The regulator for retail financial services is the Personal Investment Authority: Hertsmere House, Hertsmere Road, London E14 4AB. Tel: (020) 7216 0016.

LEGAL SERVICES

Complaints must first be made to the relevant professional body, e.g. the Office for the Supervision of Solicitors. If unsatisfied, try the Legal Services Ombudsman: Victoria Court, 8 Dormer Place, Leamington Spa, Warwickshire CV32 5AE. Tel: (01926) 822 007/8/9.

MORTGAGES

The industry is currently self-regulated but the Government proposes to introduce controls over mortgage lenders (but not advisers) through the FSA, around mid 2001.

PENSIONS

The Occupational Pensions Advisory Service (OPAS) helps with problems regarding occupational or personal pensions. You need to write (after taking the matter as far as you can with the pension provider) to: 11 Belgrave Road, London SW1V 1RB. Tel: (020) 7233 8080.

Unresolved complaints can be referred to the Pensions Ombudsman who is at the same address as OPAS but not otherwise connected, and with a different telephone number: (020) 7834 9144.

Pension fund managers are regulated by IMRO, see above under investments.

TAX AND NATIONAL INSURANCE CONTRIBUTIONS

Complain first to the officer-in-charge at your office. If not satisfied, write to the appropriate Controller (see leaflet IR120). Finally, there is the Revenue Adjudicator: Haymarket House, 28 Haymarket, London SW1Y 4SP. Tel: (020) 7930 2292.

Glossary

Actuary. Qualified person who understands life expectancy and similar matters and so can calculate the contributions required for the benefits specified.

AITC. Association of Investment Trust Companies.

All-employee share scheme. A new tax-efficient share option scheme.

All-share index. An index of all shares quoted on the London Stock Exchange.

Annual equivalent rate (AER). Interest rate received by a lender which takes account of the timing of payments, in order to be fully comparable.

Annual percentage rate (APR). A rate of interest paid on a loan which takes account of the timing of payments and any related charges.

Annuity. A guaranteed income for life, purchased with a lump sum. Part of the income is interest and part is repayment of capital.

APCIMS. The Association of Private Client Investment Managers and Stockbrokers.

Approved personal pension (APP). A personal pension which can be contracted out of SERPs.

Assessment. Calculation or estimate of tax payable.

AUTIF. Association of Unit Trusts and Investment Funds.

AVC. Additional voluntary contribution to a pension scheme.

Bank of England brokerage service. A service for personal investors to buy, hold and sell gilts, as an alternative to the Stock Exchange.

Base rate. The interest rate fixed by the Bank of England which effectively controls all UK interest rates.

Bed and ISAing. Same as bed and breakfasting, except that the shares are bought back into an ISA (still permitted).

CATs. Standards for ISAs (and mortgages from mid 2001).

CGT. Capital gains tax.

Code number. Number used for income tax on employees, to spread annual allowances (and any annual deductions) evenly over the year.

Company share option scheme. Share option scheme limited to selected employees, which can enjoy tax advantages.

Compulsory purchase annuity (CPA). The annuity which must be purchased from a personal pension scheme on retirement.

Contracted out. Not paying National Insurance contributions to or receiving benefits from SERPS.

Crest. A new system of share transactions where the shares are registered in the name of a nominee company.

Debentures. Company fixed interest stocks which are secured on some or all of the assets of the company.

Deductible or excess. Insurance term for self-insurance up to a maximum amount.

Deed of variation. Amendment of a will after death, with agreement of all beneficiaries.

Deferred pension. A pension left behind in an occupational scheme, payable from some date in the future, usually the normal retirement date for the scheme.

Early retirement factor (ERF). An amount (usually an annual percentage) by which a pension is reduced for earlier payment.

Earnings per share (EPS). Profit for a period divided by the number of shares in issue.

EIS. Enterprise investment scheme.

Enterprise management incentives. A new share option scheme for key employees in smaller companies.

Equities. Ordinary stocks and shares in companies.

Escalation. Annual increase in a pension in payment.

Face value. The issue value of a stock (may be the same as the redemption value).

Final salary scheme. A pension scheme in which the pension is based on the salary immediately before retirement.

Friendly society. A mutual insurance and savings organisation operating for the benefit of its members.

FSA. Financial Services Authority (previously called SIB).

FSAVC. Free-standing AVC, i.e. an AVC outside the company pension scheme.

FT/SE 100 index. The index of equity shares in the 100 companies on the London Stock Exchange with the largest market capitalisation.

Gearing. The ability of an investment trust to borrow money to invest, thus gearing up or increasing the opportunity for growth and/or income increase (and the risk of loss).

Gilts (or gilt-edged). British government fixed interest stocks. Interest on some is index-linked.

Giro. Banking system operated by Alliance & Leicester Building Society. Transactions can be carried out at any post office.

Graduated pension. An additional State pension which applied before SERPS was introduced, i.e. between 1961 and 1975.

Gross. Interest paid gross is paid before deduction of tax.

Growth. The increase in value of an equity investment.

Guaranteed minimum pension (GMP). The minimum pension which must be paid by a contracted-out scheme up till 1997.

ICT. Immediately chargable transfers.

ISA. Individual savings account.

IFA. Independent financial adviser.

IHT. Inheritance tax.

IMRO. Investment Managers Regulatory Organisation.

Index-linked. Varying in accordance with the retail price index, which measures inflation.

Index tracking. Investments which are linked to an index, usually the FT/SE 100 or the all-share index.

Intestacy rules. Rules for sharing out an estate in the absence of a will.

Investment trust. A company whose business is the buying, holding and selling of shares.

IR. Inland Revenue.

LISA. Lifetime individual savings account. A possible alternative to personal pensions.

Loan stock. Company fixed interest stock, usually unsecured.

LSE. The London Stock Exchange.

Marginal tax rate. The top rate you pay on your income and therefore the rate you pay on any additional taxable income or what you save on any income reduction.

Money-purchase. The type of pension scheme in which the contributions are fixed and the benefits vary.

NAPF. National Association of Pension Funds.

National Savings. British government scheme for borrowing money directly from the public.

Negative equity. Where the value of the property has fallen below the outstanding balance of the mortgage.

Net asset value (NAV). The market value of the underlying investments of an investment trust.

Non-joiner. A new employee who decides not to join the employers' pension scheme.

OCEA. Ombudsman for Corporate Estate Agents.

Oeic. Open-ended investment company, a new form of unit trust, which has only one price for buying and selling, and charges are separate.

OPAS. Occupational Pensions Advisory Service.

OPB. Occupational Pensions Board.

Open market option. Where the provider of a personal pension allows an annuity to be bought from someone else.

Opt-out. A decision by an existing employee to leave an employers' pension scheme in favour of a personal pension.

Ordinary share. Share in a company which receives dividends out of profits left after paying any interest and preference dividend.

Par value. The nominal value of a share (may be the same as the issue value).

PAYE. Pay-as-you-earn system of income tax for employees.

PEP. Personal equity plan.

P/E ratio. Share price divided by earnings (profit after tax) per share.

PET. Potentially exempt transfer, under inheritance tax.

PIA. Personal Investment Authority.

Pound/cost averaging. A mathematical advantage from regular investment in equities.

Preference share. A share in a company which receives a fixed dividend out of profit, usually before any dividend on the ordinary shares.

Purchased life annuity (PLA). An annuity purchased voluntarily.

Redemption. Repayment, usually of a capital sum at the end of the investment period.

Redemption yield. Yield which also takes into account the difference between current market price and redemption value, allowing for the time to redemption.

Rights issues. The issue by a company of further shares for cash to existing shareholders.

Rolling up. When income is kept in an investment instead of being paid out.

Save-as-you-earn (SAYE). Contract with a building society to save up to £250 a month for at least three years, tax free, in connection with a share option scheme.

Savings-related share option scheme. An employee share option scheme associated with a save-as-you-earn contract.

Scrip dividend. The opportunity to take new shares instead of a cash dividend.

Self-assessment. New system of tax returns for self-employed and certain employees.

SERPS. The State additional pension (sometimes called the State earnings-related pension scheme, hence SERPs).

SETS. Stock exchange electronic trading system, also called order-driven trading. A new system of electronic trading in FT/SE 100 shares, whereby buyers and sellers are automatically matched.

SFA. Securities and Futures Authority.

Sharesave. Another name for a savings-related share option scheme.

SHIP. Society for Home Income Plans.

SSP. Second State Pension, replacing SERPS in April 2002.

SSP. Statutory sick pay paid by an employer for a limited period.

Stakeholder pension. New form of pension scheme being introduced in April 2001.

Stop-loss. A set price for a share held, at a percentage below the purchase price, to signal the need to consider selling in order to limit any loss.

Taxable. Income paid gross but subject to tax.

Taxed. Income which is taxed at source, i.e. before payment.

Tenants-in-common. A form of property ownership whereby each party (e.g. each spouse) owns part outright.

TESSA. Tax-exempt special savings account.

Unit trust. A pool of funds managed by a professional company but owned separately by a trust.

VCT. Venture capital trust.

Written in trust. An arrangement to keep the proceeds of a life assurance policy out of the deceased's estate.

Yield. The return on an investment (interest or dividend) expressed as a percentage of the market value.

Index